José Merino & Susan T

Cuaderno de ejercicios en inglés

Práctica de gramática y estructuras

English Grammar & Structure Practice

Third Edition

> The image used on the cover of this book is from Corel Professional Photos CD-Rom: London, England.

© José Merino Bustamante y Susan Taylor

Reservados los derechos para todos los países. De conformidad con lo dispuesto en el artículo 534-bis del Código Penal vigente, podrán ser castigados con penas de multa y privación de libertad quienes reprodujeren o plagiaren, en todo o en parte, una obra literaria, artística o científica fijada en cualquier tipo de soporte sin la preceptiva autorización. Ninguna parte de esta publicación, incluído el diseño de la cubierta, puede ser reproducida, almacenada o transmitida de ninguna forma, ni por ningún medio, sea éste electrónico, químico, mecánico, electro-óptico, grabación, fotocopia o cualquier otro, sin la previa autorización escrita por parte de la Editorial.

Editorial Anglo Didáctica, S.L.
C/ Santiago de Compostela, 16
28034 Madrid – Spain.
Tel: 91 378 01 88.

ISBN: 84-86623-83-9
Depósito legal: M. 17.904-2000

Imprenta Fareso, S. A.
Paseo de la Dirección, 5
28039 Madrid

Impreso en España.
Printed in Spain.

Anglo-Didáctica Publishing

PRESENTACION

Este cuaderno de trabajo se compone de una colección muy variada de 140 ejercicios, con sus soluciones, con objeto de practicar diversos puntos lingüísticos de la lengua inglesa. En él se estudia el uso u omisión de los artículos; se repasan los sustantivos y los adjetivos; se revisan los pronombres; se ejercitan los verbos en sus diferentes aspectos; se aclara la diferencia entre adverbios y adjetivos; se practican preposiciones y conjunciones, y se hace hincapié en el orden de las palabras en la frase inglesa.

Estos ejercicios son imprescindibles para adquirir la soltura necesaria para la comunicación tanto oral como escrita, pues sirven para repasar y profundizar en los puntos importantes para el hispanohablante.

Puede usarse este cuaderno de ejercicios como complemento de cualquier libro de texto o método de inglés, ya que el vocabulario empleado y los puntos que en él se tratan son de uso común.

Los autores.

Anglo-Didáctica Publishing

INDICE

	Ejercicio nº	Página
ARTICULOS	1 al 3	5
SUSTANTIVOS	4 al 12	7
SUSTANTIVOS / ADJETIVOS	13	10
ADJETIVOS	14 al 19	10
PRONOMBRES	20 al 34	13
ADJETIVOS / PRONOMBRES	35 al 37	20
VERBOS	38 al 82	22
ADVERBIOS	83 al 95	45
ADVERBIOS / ADJETIVOS	96 al 98	52
PREPOSICIONES	99 al 119	54
CONJUNCIONES	120 al 124	63
GENITIVO SAJON	125 al 126	65
ORDEN DE LAS PALABRAS	127 al 137	66
ESTILO DIRECTO / INDIRECTO	138 al 139	71
EXCLAMACIONES	140	72
ANSWER KEY		73

1

ARTICULOS. Colóquese el artículo indeterminado *a / an* donde sea preciso. Donde no lo sea, indíquese con un aspa (X).

1. I have lessons twice .... week.
2. There are .... hundred pencils in that box.
3. I have .... news for your father.
4. Tom is such .... good boy.
5. My brother is .... teacher.
6. I am in .... hurry. I can't stop now.
7. What .... nasty weather!
8. This is .... hard work.
9. Betty has .... good memory.
10. I only ate half .... apple.
11. Playing chess is .... great fun.
12. The scouts lit .... fire to keep themselves warm.
13. What .... good beer!
14. My father is looking for .... employment.
15. Bob is reading .... English book.
16. You're making .... great progress in French.
17. Robert hasn't .... car.
18. The children are making .... noise.
19. Your sister has .... lovely hair.
20. I usually drive at 45 miles .... hour.

2

ARTICULOS. Colóquese el artículo determinado *the* donde sea necesario. Donde no lo sea, indíquese con un aspa (X).

1. At what time do they serve .... dinner?
2. She usually stays in .... bed till eleven o'clock.
3. Can you play .... violin?
4. My shirt is on .... bed.
5. .... Doctor Evans isn't in Madrid now.
6. .... dinner they gave us was delicious.
7. .... English drink tea.
8. I spoke to her .... last night.
9. My little daughter goes to .... new school near the park.
10. Did you see .... Buckingham Palace when you were in London?
11. .... zebra is an animal that looks something like a horse.

12. .... water consists of hydrogen and oxygen.
13. We'll go to London .... next week.
14. .... life is hard.
15. .... dogs bark.
16. I saw Tim at .... airport
17. There's a nice picture on .... page 29.
18. This is a book about the life of .... insects.
19. Look at .... sky.
20. .... children who live next door are very obedient.

3

ARTICULOS. Colóquense los artículos *the, a / an* donde sea necesario. Donde no lo sea, indíquese señalándolo con un aspa (X).

1. When we were in London, we visited .... Westminster Abbey.
2. .... lesson will begin at 4 pm.
3. Today is .... holiday.
4. John Smith is .... engineer.
5. Mr Evans is very good as .... teacher.
6. My little daughter has .... temperature.
7. Come on, tell us .... truth.
8. At what time do you have .... breakfast?
9. We'll see you on .... Sunday!
10. We go to .... school every day.
11. When .... iron gets old, it rusts.
12. I can't write without .... pen.
13. There's no smoke without .... fire.
14. The boy threw .... stone at the dog.
15. This table is made of .... wood.
16. .... English is spoken in Great Britain.
17. I like .... colour of your jacket.
18. .... factories have tall chimneys.
19. .... factories in my town have very tall chimneys.
20. .... sheep gives milk.

4

SUSTANTIVOS. Escríbanse estas frases, sustituyendo los sustantivos del género femenino (en cursiva) por masculino.

1. Where's your *niece*?
2. My *mother* is in London.
3. I'm a *waitress*.
4. Is there a *lioness* in the zoo?
5. My *aunt* is coming today.
6. That *woman* is a *witch*.
7. I've just seen your *sister*.
8. There's a *lady* asking for her.
9. My *grandmother* is seventy.

5

SUSTANTIVOS. Sustitúyanse los sustantivos del género masculino (en cursiva) por femenino, haciendo los cambios adicionales necesarios.

1. The *king* is speaking now.
2. He is a *hero*.
3. The *manservant* is there.
4. My *husband* is sitting on that chair.
5. The *boys* are waiting.
6. He is a *widower*.
7. My *father* is speaking to the *landlord*.
8. This is my *uncle* and this is his *son*.
9. The *earl* was born here.
10. There are two *bulls* on that farm.

6

SUSTANTIVOS. Dígase cuáles son los opuestos -masculino o femenino- de estos sustantivos.

1. Master ....
2. Niece ....
3. Actor ....
4. Tigress ....
5. God ....
6. Nun ....
7. Lad ....
8. Hen ....
9. Bridegroom ....
10. Princess ....

7

SUSTANTIVOS. Indíquese cuál es el plural de los siguientes sustantivos.

1. Brother-in-law...............
2. Armchair......................
3. Oasis............................
4. Phenomenon ....
5. Woman student ....
6. Child............................
7. Tooth ....
8. Safe.............................
9. Thief............................
10. Army...........................
11. Piano..........................
12. Potato.........................
13. Bridge ....
14. Dish ....
15. Hero...........................
16. Photo.........................
17. Key ....
18. Life ....
19. Roof ....
20. Goose........................

8

SUSTANTIVOS. Entre estos 14 sustantivos, hay 4 que no cambian en plural. Subráyense.

salmon, chief, dish, bus, calf, ship, echo, louse, foot, sheep, tree, deer, trout, volcano.

9

SUSTANTIVOS. Escríbanse las frases siguientes, cambiando los sustantivos en plural por singular.

1. Birds fly..
2. Boys play..
3. Dogs bark. ....
4. Cows give milk. ....
5. Cats have four legs. ....
6. Bakers sell bread. ....
7. Horses gallop. ....
8. Postmen deliver letters. ....
9. Children cry. ....
10. Men go to work..................................

10
SUSTANTIVOS. Escríbanse las frases siguientes, cambiando al plural los sustantivos que aparecen en letra cursiva. En algunos casos, hay que hacer algunos cambios adicionales para que las frases tengan sentido.

1. There's a *piano* in that room.
2. Look, there's a *fly* on the ceiling.
3. The *knife* is on that table.
4. The *man* came with his *wife*.
5. My *child* has just come home from school.
6. I can see a *sheep* in that field.
7. The *watch* was in the box.
8. The *ox* was near the farm.
9. The books are on that *shelf*.
10. I've caught a *trout*.
11. The boy sent a *letter* without a *stamp* on it.
12. Is this a *glass*?
13. Is there a *lady* in the shop?
14. That *boy* wants to go to Liverpool.
15. This is a *mouse*.

11
SUSTANTIVOS. Complétese cada definición o descripción, escribiendo un sustantivo compuesto en las líneas de puntos.

1. A room in which meals are eaten is a ....
2. A piece of furniture for keeping books in is a ....
3. A cup used for drinking tea is a ....
4. A person who steals from people's pockets is a ....
5. A printed publication issued every day with news is a ....
6. A window in a shop where goods are shown is a ....
7. A stick of colouring material used by women to put on their lips is a ....
8. A married woman responsible for the home where she lives is a ....
9. A shop where shoes are sold is a ....
10. A person who tells someone's fortune is a ....

12

SUSTANTIVOS. Tradúzcanse estas frases, empleando sustantivos que pueden o no contarse.

1. Os voy a dar un consejo.
2. No hay muchos muebles en aquella habitación.
3. Tom ha hecho progresos en español.
4. Tengo una noticia interesante para ti.
5. Aprender inglés es un trabajo duro.
6. He desayunado tostadas con mantequilla.
7. Mi hermana tiene buenos conocimientos de alemán.

13

SUSTANTIVOS / ADJETIVOS. Usense los adjetivos siguientes como sustantivos en los espacios punteados.

rich   poor   sick   ambitious   dumb
English   French   Welsh   blind

1. The .... can't see.
2. The rich must help the ....
3. A nurse takes care of the ....
4. There are plenty of opportunities for the ....
5. The .... drive on the left; the .... on the right.
6. The .... live in a country to the west of England.
7. The .... are not always happy.
8. The .... can't speak.

14

ADJETIVOS. Complétense estas frases con adjetivos en su forma comparativa, p. ej. *Mount Aconcagua is high, but Mount Everest is higher.*

1. The Ebro is long, but the Tajo is ....
2. My tea is hot, but yours is ....
3. The bank is big, but the hotel is ....
4. My grandfather is old, but Mr Wilson is ....
5. Johnny is strong, but my cousin Peter is ....
6. Your car is good, but mine is ....
7. This exercise is easy, but that one is ....

8. It is cold today, but it was .... yesterday.
9. Mr Benson is thin, but Mr Lodge is ....
10. My luggage is heavy, but yours is ....

15

ADJETIVOS. Escríbanse estas frases, empleando el adjetivo, que aparece entre paréntesis, en forma comparativa o superlativa, según sea el caso.

1. Joan is the (pretty) girl in the class.
2. Philip is (intelligent) than his cousin.
3. This chair isn't (comfortable) as the sofa.
4. The Nile is (long) than the Ebro.
5. June is (warm) than April.
6. This is the (bad) film we have ever seen.
7. Is Joe (tall) as you are?
8. Jake is the (good) footballer in the country.
9. This is the (important) day in my life.
10. These cigarettes are (good) than those.

16

ADJETIVOS. De acuerdo con las aseveraciones siguientes, fórmense oraciones en las que aparezcan adjetivos en forma comparativa. Hay que formar la frase con los adjetivos que se dan entre paréntesis, p. ej. *I have £3,000. You have £2,000 (rich). Solución: I am richer than you.* En algunos casos, también se da la palabra con la que debe comenzar la frase.

1. John is 21 years old. James is 21 years old, too. (old)
2. The river is 2 miles long. The road is 2 miles long, too. (long)
3. Charles is 6 feet tall. Tony is 5 feet tall. (tall)
4. The park has 3,000 square meters. The field has 2,000 square meters. (The park / big)
5. The piano weighs 200 pounds. The box weighs 200 pounds. (heavy)
6. Mr Brown has £1,000. Mr Smith has £2,000. Mr Carter has £3,000. (Mr Carter / rich)
7. Sun Street is 200 yards long. Moon Street is 300 yards long. High Street is 100 yards long. (Moon Street / long)
8. The river is 10 yards wide. The street is 8 yards wide. The road is 6 yards wide. (The river / wide)

9. The pond is 3 feet deep. The river is 5 feet deep. (deep)
10. This car can go at 100 miles an hour. That motor-cycle can go at 90 miles an hour. (The car / fast)

17

ADJETIVOS. Complétense los espacios en blanco con la forma apropiada de los adjetivos que aparecen entre paréntesis, de acuerdo con los datos que se dan en cada caso. Además, es necesario añadir alguna palabra adicional para completar la frase.

a) *The book weighs 2 pounds. The box weighs 2 pounds, too. The packet only weighs 1 pound.*

1. The book is .... the packet. (heavy)
2. The box is .... the book. (heavy)
3. The packet is .... the book. (heavy)
4. The packet is .... the box. (light)
5. The packet is .... of all. (light)

b) *The blue car costs £1,000. The red car costs £500. The green one costs £200.*

6. The blue car is .... the red one. (expensive)
7. The green car is .... the red one. (expensive)
8. The blue car is .... of all. (expensive)
9. The red car is .... the blue one. (cheap)
10. The green car is .... of all. (cheap)

18

ADJETIVOS. Complétense estas oraciones con los adjetivos apropiados, según el contexto.

1. He isn't .... enough to reach the apples on the tree.
2. When your hair is too .... you must have it cut.
3. Betty's dress is as .... as snow.
4. Your hands are .... Go and wash them.
5. I don't need to wash my hands. They are ....
6. A widow is a woman whose husband is ....
7. The .... part of the foot is called the heel.
8. Don Quixote was thin, but Sancho Panza was ....
9. He isn't .... He's only thirty-five.

10. It is .... in winter.

19

ADJETIVOS. Tradúzcanse las oraciones siguientes al inglés. Se han de emplear adjetivos compuestos.

1. Mi padre es un hombre muy distraído.
2. Jack es un chico muy trabajador.
3. El llevaba un traje azul oscuro.
4. Una mujer bien vestida entró en la habitación y se sentó.
5. Hay un chico de aspecto sucio esperándote.

20

PRONOMBRES. En cada espacio punteado, escríbase un pronombre personal, de forma que la frase tenga sentido, p. ej. *Did you speak to Tim? - Yes, I spoke to him.*

1. Is this your friends' car? - Yes, it belongs to ....
2. Alice, Mary, where are you? - .... are here in this room.
3. Where is your mother? - .... is in the kitchen.
4. The boy said, "Please show .... that comic."
5. Are you speaking to your sister on the telephone? - Yes, I'm speaking to ....
6. The children said, "Please, give .... some money to buy sweets."
7. Where are Tim and Joe? - .... are in Rome now.
8. Peggy, Betty, does this dog belong to you? - Yes, it belongs to ....
9. Whose are those books? - .... are mine.
10. Do you all understand the teacher? - Yes, ... understand him.
11. He is in front of the table. The table is behind ....
12. .... am behind Mr Norton. Mr Norton is in front of ....
13. There's a picture of a castle on page 30. Look at ....
14. Are you talking to me? - Yes, I'm talking to ....
15. You will not be able to see .... tomorrow because we shall be away.

21

PRONOMBRES. Escríbanse de nuevo estas frases, sustituyendo las palabras que aparecen escritas en letra cursiva por pronombres personales.

1. *Peter and Robert* go to school.
2. I was in front of *the old woman*.
3. *Mr Norton* is a very good doctor.
4. *My daughter* is in the dining-room.
5. The teacher is among *the students*.
6. *Tom and I* are students.
7. *The car* is in the car park.
8. I am behind *my brother*.
9. Send *Tim and me* as many books as you can.
10. Where are *the students*?
11. I saw *Jean's parents* yesterday.
12. Give *Peggy* a cup of tea.
13. Put *your books* on the table.
14. Put *your book* on the table.
15. When is *Bruce* going to visit *Molly*?

22

PRONOMBRES. Escójanse y subráyense, en cada una de las frases que se proponen, los pronombres personales que sean adecuados.

1. (We / Us) write to (they / them) every month.
2. (Me / I) called (him / he) last night.
3. (She / Her) talked to (us / we) last week.
4. Don't listen to (he / him).
5. (Them / They) asked (we / us) about (she / her).
6. That's Mrs Wilson. Give (her / she) an umbrella.
7. Has anyone asked for (I / me)?
8. Have you paid my brother? - Yes, I've paid (he / him).
9. Did (him / he) speak to you yesterday?
10. Whose cigarettes are these? - (Them / They) are my father's.

23

PRONOMBRES. Complétense las oraciones siguientes con los pronombres posesivos apropiados.

1. This is our farm. It is ....
2. These are my sister's gloves. They are ....
3. This is your tea. It is ....
4. I have a dictionary. It is ....
5. They have a house. It is ....
6. This dress belongs to my mother. It is ....
7. These books belong to Tim and Mary. They are ....
8. This is my father's desk. It is ....
9. Mr and Mrs Benson live here. This house is ....
10. Jack is driving a car. It is ....

24

PRONOMBRES. Complétense las oraciones siguientes con los pronombres reflexivos o recíprocos adecuados. En algunos casos, los pronombres reflexivos están utilizados en sentido enfático.

1. Listen, Peter is talking to ....
2. Why didn't you speak up for ....?
3. I live by ....
4. The children amused .... all evening.
5. Pete, Joe, you must do your exercises ....
6. Did Dorothy hurt .... when she fell?
7. The dog is scratching ....
8. I looked at .... in the mirror.
9. Did you both enjoy .... at the party?
10. You mustn't praise ....
11. Help Pete with his exercises. He can't do them by ....
12. Those five men hate ....
13. The two sisters love ....
14. They all gave books to ....
15. The two boys looked at .... and said nothing.

25

PRONOMBRES. En los espacios punteados, colóquese el pronombre interrogativo adecuado para formular correctamente las preguntas.

Who   Whose   Which   What

1. .... came last week? - Peter did.
2. .... did you open the door with? - I opened it with this key.
3. .... did you go to the cinema with? - I went to the cinema with my brother.
4. .... daughter are you?
5. .... of these umbrellas do you prefer?
6. .... are you thinking about? - I'm thinking about my holiday.
7. .... is that bag? It's the teacher's.
8. .... of these cases is yours?
9. .... gave you that money?
10. .... did you see walking in the park?

26

PRONOMBRES. Para cada una de estas respuestas, formúlese una pregunta que comience por un pronombre interrogativo, de acuerdo con las palabras en cursiva que aparecen en las respuestas.

Who   Whose   Which   What

1. ....? -This is *Tim's* bicycle.
2. ....? -*Mr Williams* is here today.
3. ....? -I have written the letter with *this pen*.
4. ....? -I saw *Peter* at the station.
5. ....? -I like *the blue blouse* best.
6. ....? -*The children* played in the garden.
7. ....? -I bought *this book*.
8. ....? -*My father* helped me.
9. ....? -It's *my* cap.
10. ....? -Let's *go for a walk* now.

27

PRONOMBRES. Vuélvase a escribir cada una de estas oraciones, colocando el pronombre interrogativo en primer lugar y pasando la preposición al final. Obsérvese el cambio que sufre el pronombre *whom* en el lenguaje corriente.

1. To whom did he speak?
2. With what did you open the tin?
3. To which of these hotels did they go?
4. With whom did you go to the theatre?
5. About what are you talking?
6. To whom did you send the letter?
7. About what is he thinking?
8. At whom did he look?
9. From whom did you receive those flowers?
10. For whom are you waiting?

28

PRONOMBRES. Unase cada par de frases mediante un pronombre relativo (*who* o *which*), p. ej. *The girl is my niece. She was here last night* pasa a ser: *The girl who was here last night is my niece.* A veces son posibles dos respuestas.

1. The dog is not mine. It is barking.
2. The woman is Mrs Williams. She is singing.
3. The parrot is beautiful. It is speaking.
4. The boy is my cousin. He broke the window.
5. The cat belongs to Mrs Carter. It always sleeps in that basket.
6. The students are in that classroom. They study geography.
7. The traveller is very old. He tells interesting stories.
8. The old man travelled all over the world. He lives here now.
9. The station-master stopped the train. He has a blue cap.
10. The horse is white. It won the race last week.

29

PRONOMBRES. Insértense en estas frases los pronombres relativos *who* o *which*. En el caso en que el pronombre relativo no sea preciso, indíquese marcándolo con un aspa (X).

1. The book .... I bought in London is very interesting.
2. The boy .... I met in the street is Philip's cousin.
3. The dog .... is eating a bone belongs to Arthur.

4. The man .... is speaking to your aunt is Mr Carter.
5. Those are the cats .... catch mice.
6. That's the woman .... sells butter and cheese.
7. These are the girls .... study English.
8. Those are the students .... I know.
9. The book .... has 300 pages belongs to Mr Parker.
10. The horse .... won the race is black.

30

PRONOMBRES. Vuélvase a escribir cada oración, omitiendo el pronombre relativo y colocando la preposición al final, p. ej. *That's the film about which I am talking* **pasa a ser:** *That's the film I am talking about.*

1. These are the fishermen to whom we always talk.
2. Those are the fishing-boats about which they were speaking.
3. That's the bus in which I go to school.
4. This is the picture at which I am looking.
5. That's the man to whom I lent the money.
6. This is the hotel in which we stayed.
7. That's the glass from which he used to drink wine.
8. Those are the ladies with whom my sister lives.
9. This is the record to which I listened.
10. That's the chair on which he sat.

31

PRONOMBRES. Vuélvase a escribir cada una de estas oraciones, omitiendo el pronombre relativo y el verbo *to be***, p. ej. la frase:** *The dictionary that is on the shelf is mine* **pasa a ser:** *The dictionary on the shelf is mine.*

1. The sheep that are in that field give good wool.
2. The swans that are on the pond are very beautiful.
3. The horse that is under that tree is eating grass.
4. The man that is by the traffic lights is a policeman.
5. The students that are in that classroom are studying French.
6. The vase that is on the table is very fragile.
7. The car that is in the garage is mine.
8. The apples that are in that basket are ripe.
9. The children that are in the park are playing football.

10. The glasses that are in the cupboard are dirty.
11. The shirt that is on the bed is mine.
12. The tickets that are in this envelope are for you.

32

PRONOMBRES. En cada una de las siguientes oraciones propuestas faltan dos pronombres. Elíjanse los que sean apropiados para completarlas y escríbanse en los espacios punteados.

something anything nobody none some anyone nothing

1. What did you do during the holiday? .... at all. - I just wanted to relax, and didn't feel like doing ....!
2. Is .... using that computer? - No, ... is using it at the moment.
3. I'm hungry. I'd like .... to eat, but I don't want .... to drink, thank you.
4. Are you sure you wouldn't like .... to drink? - No, ... at all, thank you.
5. Can .... here speak English? - No, ... at all.
6. .... of the students speak Spanish, but none of them speak English.
7. There's somebody downstairs! I can hear a noise! - Don't be silly, there's .... there!
8. What shall we have for dinner? Do you want something special? - Oh, I don't mind. .... you like, you choose!

33

PRONOMBRES. Complétense estas oraciones, escribiendo en cada uno de los espacios punteados el pronombre indefinido apropiado. Escójase entre los siguientes:

nobody anything nothing something everyone one

1. I have no money, so I can't buy ....
2. There is .... like drinking good whisky.
3. The boy went into the room so silently that .... heard him.
4. I'd like .... to eat. I'm quite hungry.
5. The blind can't see ....
6. Is there anything in that drawer? -Yes, there's .... in there. There's a handkerchief.

7. .... in Great Britain knows who Shakespeare was.
8. .... can never be sure.
9. There's .... in this box. It is empty.
10. I have .... to do today, so I'm going to the cinema.

34

PRONOMBRES. Vuélvanse a escribir las oraciones siguientes, empleando el pronombre *one(s)* en vez de los sustantivos que se repiten en la misma línea.

1. The red book is on the teacher's desk and the blue book is here.
2. This is a strong cigarette and that is a mild cigarette.
3. This car is small and that car is big.
4. There were apples in the basket, good apples and bad apples.
5. Here are two drawers. Fill the empty drawer.
6. Do you prefer this armchair or the armchair by the window?
7. Did you wear the old jumper? -No, I wore the new jumper.
8. I like westerns. -Did you see the western they showed last week?
9. She doesn't like white shoes. She likes brown shoes.
10. These photos are not as good as the photos your brother took last year.

35

ADJETIVOS / PRONOMBRES. Escríbanse los adjetivos o pronombres posesivos de acuerdo con el contexto de la frase.

1. Betty put .... coat on and went out.
2. Betty, put .... coat on! It's cold outside.
3. It was given to her by .... own mother.
4. Is this your book? -Yes, it's .... book.
5. Is this my book? -Yes, it's .... book
6. That ball-pen isn't yours. It's .... because she bought it.
7. This is Andrew and this is .... car.
8. This money is all .... My father gave it to me.
9. Philip, Tim, where are your caps? -.......... caps are on that chair.
10. The little rabbit has hurt .... leg.
11. Is this your camera? - No, it isn't ....
12. We have our hats and they have ....
13. Joe has his case and Alice has ....
14. They are in their house and we are in ....
15. Are those Joe's socks? -Yes, they are ....
16. Is that .... cat? - No, my cat is bigger.

17. This is my dog and this is .... collar.
18. These are my friends and that is .... father.
19. Is this .... watch? -Yes, it is yours.
20. This is my niece and that is .... scarf.

36

ADJETIVOS / PRONOMBRES. Elíjase el adjetivo o pronombre posesivo / personal / reflexivo apropiado en cada caso y escríbase en la línea de puntos.

1. I want to give .... my book.
   (her / she / herself)
2. Do .... dress yourself in the bathroom?
   (your / yours / you)
3. I use .... car every day.
   (mine / my / myself)
4. Mr Armstrong says the hat is ....
   (himself / him / his)
5. Whose gloves are these? -They belong to ....
   (my / myself / me)
6. The boys want to speak about ....
   (their / theirs / themselves)
7. Pamela is looking at .... in the mirror.
   (her / herself / hers)
8. Is this your house? -Yes, it is ....
   (our / ours / us)
9. I'm not talking to her. I'm talking to ....
   (your / you / yours)
10. I'm sure this notebook belongs to ....
    (him / his / he)

37

ADJETIVOS / PRONOMBRES. En las frases que siguen, insértese una de estas palabras, las cuales pueden tener el doble valor de adjetivos o pronombres.

*much both each little most few all
either neither another others*

1. The teacher gave a dictionary to .... student.
2. They have very .... money. They are poor.

3. As it rained hard, ... people went to watch the football match.
4. .... men are mortal.
5. Hurry up! we don't have .... time.
6. He has written two novels and I've read .... of them.
7. Not all my English friends speak Spanish, but .... do.
8. Many students study English, but very .... speak it well.
9. .... people study Old English except at university.
10. They haven't .... money. They are not rich.
11. I don't like this song. Please sing ....
12. Will you have .... piece of cake?
13. I don't like any of these ties. Do you have any ....?
14. The teacher gave me two pens, but .... is very good.
15. There are trees on .... side of the road.

38

VERBOS. Vuélvanse a escribir estas oraciones en negativo, haciendo los cambios necesarios.

1. You have a lot of fish on your plate.
2. She has told me the news.
3. They came last night.
4. She bought some bread this morning.
5. I want to go abroad for my holidays.
6. They studied French last year.
7. He catches a bus to go to work.
8. We are going to eat meat for lunch.
9. I think she's intelligent.
10. He has a lot of friends in London.

39

VERBOS. Cámbiense estas frases a interrogativo.

1. They are going to leave at 10 o'clock.
2. He caught a bus this morning.
3. She studies her lessons in the afternoon.
4. My father ate some fish for lunch.
5. Your mother bought some sweets for Betty.
6. He understands me.
7. My sister comes to class every day.
8. He smokes a pipe after lunch.

9. Your brother has a lot of friends in this town.
10. Mr Evans eats a lot of meat.

40

VERBOS. Complétense estas preguntas de forma que se correspondan con las respuestas que se dan.

1. .... speak English? - Yes, he can.
2. .... come last week? - No, she didn't.
3. .... know her? - Yes, he does.
4. .... seen them? - No, I haven't.
5. .... catch the bus this morning? - Yes, I did.
6. .... Spanish? - No, I'm not.
7. .... see you at the station? - Yes, they did.
8. .... got any money? - No, we haven't.
9. .... stop the car by the bank? - Yes, I did.
10. .... smoke? - No, I don't.

41

VERBOS. Formúlense las preguntas apropiadas, de acuerdo con las expresiones en cursiva que hay en las respuestas.

1. ....? - This pencil is *for drawing*.
2. ....? - I'm interested in *music*.
3. ....? - This dog belongs to *Mr Norton*.
4. ....? - He comes from *Liverpool*.
5. ....? - I saw him *last Friday*.
6. ....? - *Let's have fish for lunch*.
7. ....? - He won't come today *because he doesn't want to*.
8. ....? - She's studying *mathematics*.
9. ....? - I put the book *on the table*.
10. ....? - They came *at ten o'clock*.

42

VERBOS. En cada espacio punteado, escríbase uno de estos imperativos.

lend take wash speak knock drive put close get type

1. .... the dictionary on that shelf.
2. .... to Mrs Carter.

3. .... the lorry.
4. .... the children to the amusement park.
5. .... into the car.
6. .... your face.
7. .... this letter.
8. .... me 1,000 pounds, please.
9. .... at the door.
10. .... the window.

43

VERBOS. Vuélvanse a escribir estas frases, cambiando el futuro de intención -una acción que se va a realizar- por el presente continuo -una acción que se está llevando a cabo- p. ej. *I'm going to write a letter* pasa a ser: *I'm writing a letter*.

1. They're going to learn English.
2. He's going to drink a cup of tea.
3. She's going to read a novel.
4. I'm going to telephone Mr Field.
5. The girls are going to play with dolls.
6. The dog is going to eat a bone.
7. We're going to watch television.
8. Philip is going to sit an exam.
9. I'm going to put on my coat.
10. My sister is going to play the violin.

44

VERBOS. Escríbanse estas frases, cambiando el verbo en *Simple Past* (pasado simple) por *Present Perfect* (pretérito perfecto), p. ej. *I wrote a book* pasa a ser: *I have written a book*.

1. Dick played chess.
2. John read a book.
3. I found my bag.
4. David spoke English.
5. She told us the truth.
6. My father smoked a pipe.
7. They bought a new flat.
8. He walked along the street.
9. I lost my money.
10. Your sister ate a cake.

45

VERBOS. Escríbase la forma adecuada del verbo que está entre paréntesis. Debe ponerse en *Simple Present* o *Present Continuous*. En algunos casos será necesario cambiar el orden de las palabras.

1. They usually (drink) coffee for breakfast, but they (not drink) coffee today.
2. (Sell) your car?
3. I (understand) the lesson now.
4. What a nice dress you (wear)!
5. It often (rain) in Galicia.
6. It (rain) hard at this moment.
7. What (do) you now? I'm looking for the ball-pen I lost this morning.
8. What (do) you for a living?
9. She usually (wear) a pink dress.
10. Wood (float).
11. Today I (go) to the cinema.
12. She (come) today.
13. I (go) to school every day.
14. We never (ask) questions.
15. The dog always (sleep) on the sofa.

46

VERBOS. Escríbase la forma correcta de cada verbo. Elíjase entre: *Simple Past, Past Continuous* o *Present Perfect*.

1. I (buy) this scarf in London.
2. I (write) the letter ten minutes ago.
3. He (live) in Manchester for two years now.
4. He (listen) to the radio when the light (go) out.
5. She (live) in New York since October.
6. We (have) breakfast when the telephone (ring).
7. Nancy (receive) a letter last week.
8. Bruce (open) the window. It is still open.
9. Tom (be) to London twice this year.
10. I (not see) him today.
11. The play (not finish) yet.
12. The children (play) in the garden yesterday.
13. I (stay) at the Princess Hotel when I was in London.
14. I already (see) that film.

15. He (drink) two glasses of wine this evening.

47

VERBOS. Escríbanse los verbos que aparecen entre paréntesis en su forma correspondiente.

1. We have (buy) a new house in Madrid.
2. You (count) the money yet?
3. I (be not) here last night.
4. The children (watch) television at this moment.
5. Last week I (find) a pound in the street.
6. I always (go) for a walk on Sundays.
7. I spoke to Jim yesterday, but I haven't (speak) to him today.
8. He (be) in London since October.
9. We (come) to Madrid an hour ago.
10. The sun didn't (shine) all day yesterday.
11. He (be) in London last month.
12. I often (see) them.
13. He (have) lunch now.
14. My father (read) the newspaper every day.
15. My father (read) the newspaper an hour ago.
16. Listen! The manager (speak).
17. We can't go out now because it (rain) hard.
18. They just (arrive)
19. We (live) in this house for a year.
20. When you (come) home? - I came home at six.
21. You (buy) this umbrella in Paris? - Yes, I did.
22. I (not know) anything about them.
23. He (not work) for a long time.
24. She (not speak) English or French.
25. Pete usually (study) his lessons in the afternoon.

48

VERBOS. Complétense estas oraciones con la forma correcta del verbo que aparece entre paréntesis. En unos casos, dicho verbo indicará acción larga *(Past Continuous)* y en otros, acción corta *(Simple Past)*.

1. While I was listening to the singer, somebody (sneeze).
2. While Johnny was crossing the street, the dog (bite) him.
3. While we were having breakfast, somebody (knock) at the door.
4. While Mr Armstrong's wife was sleeping, the baby (begin) to cry.

5. While Peggy was going along the street, she (meet) Pamela.
6. The telephone rang while Philip (write) a letter.
7. The cat ate the fish while I (shave).
8. The postman rang the bell while we (have) lunch.
9. It began to snow while they (walk) in the park.
10. There was an accident while I (wait) for the bus.

49

VERBOS. Vuélvanse a escribir estas frases, poniendo los verbos, que aparecen entre paréntesis, en *Simple Past* o *Past Continuous*, según sea adecuado.

1. When we (come) in, it (snow).
2. Last year, my daughter Betty (study) very hard.
3. Yesterday, we (play) tennis.
4. My friend Johnny (come) while I (work).
5. The class (begin) at five o'clock yesterday.
6. The students (shout) when the headmaster (enter) the classroom.
7. Peter (speak) to the teacher when I (knock) on the door.
8. When I (arrive) at class, the teacher already (give) a dictation.
9. I waited until they (finish) their dinner.
10. They (rob) the bank last night.

50

VERBOS. Contéstese a las siguientes preguntas, empleando el *Past Continuous* para indicar una acción larga, y utilizando las palabras que están entre paréntesis.

1. What were you doing at five o'clock? (write a letter).
2. What was he doing at ten o'clock? (play cards).
3. What was she doing at eleven o'clock? (go to work).
4. What were the children doing at six o'clock? (play in the garden).
5. What was Mrs Brown doing at half-past six? (make a cake).
6. What was the little girl doing at twelve o'clock? (sleep).
7. What was the teacher doing at nine o'clock? (explain the lesson).
8. What was your father doing at four o'clock? (read the newspaper).
9. What were you doing at half-past eight, John? (have a bath).
10. What were they doing at a quarter to eleven? (work).

51

VERBOS. Escríbanse estas oraciones, colocando el verbo entre paréntesis en *Past Perfect* (pretérito pluscuamperfecto).

1. When the children came back from school, she already (cook) lunch.
2. When the bell-boy came with the newspaper, Mr Wilson already (leave).
3. When they arrived at the cinema, the film already (start).
4. When we got to the station, the train already (go).
5. When I saw them in the street, I already (buy) the newspaper.
6. When the boy began to play, he already (do) his homework.
7. When Mr Evans got to the office, the manager already (call) him.
8. When my wife came back home, I already (peel) the potatoes.
9. When my brother went to England, he already (study) English.
10. When the film started, I realized that I already (see) it.

52

VERBOS. Escríbase el futuro de los verbos que aparecen entre paréntesis.

1. Tomorrow (be) Monday.
2. You (find) your gloves in that drawer.
3. We never (do) that again.
4. He (do) it whether you like it or not.
5. I (be) twenty-five tomorrow.
6. Perhaps I (go) to Paris next year.
7. If you go to London, you (see) Big Ben.
8. I (telephone) Mr Jones if I have time.
9. He (close) the door if it's cold.
10. We (not be) able to go to the theatre unless you book the seats this morning.

53

VERBOS. Practíquense las oraciones condicionales, insertando uno de los dos verbos que están entre paréntesis.

1. If you .... hard, you will earn a lot of money. (worked / work).
2. If you .... hard, you would earn a lot of money. (work / worked).

3. If he .... time, he would do the work.
   (has / had).
4. If you touch this box, it ....
   (will explode / would explode).
5. If you had worked hard, you .... tired.
   (would get / would have got).
6. If I had had enough money, I .... it.
   (would buy / would have bought).
7. If you .... the letter, we would have received it.
   (had sent / sent).
8. If it .... I would have to buy an umbrella.
   (rains / rained).
9. If it .... I will have to buy an umbrella.
   (rains / rained).
10. If you run fast, you .... the bus.
    (would catch / will catch).

54

VERBOS. Este ejercicio consiste en transformar cada una de estas oraciones, que llevan la conjunción *so,* en una oración condicional que comience por *But,* p. ej. *I didn't speak French, so I couldn't go to Paris* pasa a ser: *But if I had spoken French, I could have gone to Paris.*

1. He didn't have money, so he couldn't buy a motorbike.
   But ....
2. They didn't have a car, so they had to go by bus.
   But ....
3. We didn't work, so we didn't earn money.
   But ....
4. I didn't see him, so I didn't tell him.
   But ....
5. I didn't win the lottery, so I couldn't buy the house I wanted.
   But ....
6. We didn't finish the work on time, so we didn't get a bonus.
   But ....
7. He didn't study very hard, so he didn't get good marks in the test.
   But ....
8. They didn't park on the yellow line, so they weren't given a fine.
   But ....
9. She didn't remember to post the letter, so it won't arrive before Friday.
   But ....

10. He didn't forget to buy his wife a birthday present, so she wasn't angry.
    But ....
11. I didn't set the alarm clock, so I overslept.
    But ....
12. We didn't wear overcoats, so we felt very cold.
    But ....

55

VERBOS. Tradúzcanse estas frases, prestando atención a los subjuntivos, que aparecen en letra cursiva.

1. Te dije que *vinieras*.
2. Os daré dinero para que *vayáis* al cine.
3. Me sorprende que Tony *llegue* tan temprano hoy.
4. Es importante que *vayamos* juntos.
5. Dice que se lo dirá a ella cuando *venga*.
6. Dijo que se lo diría a ella cuando *viniera*.
7. ¡Ojalá lo *supiera*!
8. Quiero que me *corten* el pelo.
9. Esta lección es demasiado difícil para que ella la *entienda*.
10. En cuanto *llegue* Dorothy, dile que encontré su libro.

56

VERBOS. Tradúzcanse estas frases, prestando atención a los verbos reflexivos y recíprocos, que aparecen en letra cursiva.

1. Siempre *me afeito* por la mañana.
2. John y Molly *se quieren*.
3. Esos tres hombres *se odian*.
4. Ella *se está mirando* al espejo.
5. Entra y *siéntate*.
6. *Me corté* con este cuchillo.
7. *Nos perdimos* en Londres.
8. Cuando trabajo mucho *me canso*.
9. *No te preocupes*.
10. ¿*Se apea* usted en la próxima parada?

57

VERBOS. Elíjase el verbo defectivo *(Modal Verb)* apropiado. En algunos casos, es correcto más de un verbo.

*can   can't   could   couldn't   may   might   must   mustn't
shall   will   should   would   needn't   used to   ought to*

1. When I was eight, I .... play with my toys.
2. I don't know Spanish, so I .... understand him.
3. Your mother .... take an aspirin because she has a cold.
4. I .... speak English now, but I wasn't able to speak it last year.
5. Joan .... lift this box because she isn't a strong girl.
6. John .... do what he is told!
7. I .... play football when I was young.
8. He .... be Spanish because his name is Pepe.
9. I .... buy this box because I haven't any money.
10. You .... study electronics if you prefer mechanics.
11. He .... be Spanish because his name is Bruce.
12. You .... sign here, on the dotted line.
13. The heating is not working, so it .... be very cold in the house.
14. The student said, "I .... understand this lesson because it's too difficult."
15. You .... go for a walk when you have finished your homework, but not before.
16. You .... talk when the teacher is explaining the lesson.
17. I .... speak Spanish until I was eight.
18. You .... work if you want to eat.
19. It .... rain today; it's very cloudy.
20. You .... go to school tomorrow because it's a holiday.
21. Jane .... cook very well when she got married, but now she cooks wonderfully.
22. You .... overtake a car in a bend.
23. .... you cook? -Of course, I can.
24. Your father said that you .... go to the park if you wanted to.
25. What language .... you speak if you were Japanese?
26. I .... like to meet your father.
27. If you come in time, you .... see the film.
28. .... I close the door?
29. You .... help the poor.
30. .... you open the window, please?

58

VERBOS. Las llamadas *Tag Questions*, equivalentes a la expresión española "¿Verdad?", "¿No es verdad?" se forman con verbos como *be, have, do* y otros *Modal Verbs*. Este ejercicio consiste en añadir dichas *Tag Questions* en los espacios punteados, p. ej. *Today is Tuesday, isn't it?*

1. It didn't rain yesterday, ...?
2. Your name isn't Tom, ...?
3. They speak English, ...?
4. I'm Spanish, ...?
5. We live in Madrid, ...?
6. You don't drive to work, ...?
7. They've never been to China, ...?
8. He'll be on time, ...?
9. I couldn't type the letters, ...?
10. John has a car, ...?

59

VERBOS. Colóquese el verbo apropiado, según el contexto.

1. Please speak slowly. I don't .... English very well.
2. There aren't any eggs, so we can't .... an omelette.
3. I haven't any money, so I can't .... anything.
4. It's snowing hard, so I can't .... for a walk.
5. That man is deaf, so he can't .... very well.
6. She hasn't a knife, so he can't .... the bread.
7. I have got some money, so I can .... by taxi.
8. I haven't got a ball-pen, so I can't .... my address.
9. There aren't any cigarettes in that box, so I can't ....
10. I've got a record-player, so we can .... to these records.
11. My father was given a ticket, so he can .... to the football match.
12. I've bought you a typewriter, so now you can .... your letters.

60

VERBOS. Escríbase el *Modal Verb* correcto, según el contexto.

1. Good children .... obey their parents.
   (must / mustn't / needn't)

2. He's very strong, so he .... lift this piano easily.
   (can't / can / couldn't)
3. You .... come to school on Sunday.
   (mustn't / needn't / must)
4. They .... do their homework if they had time.
   (shouldn't / would / will)
5. If it .... late, I would have gone by taxi.
   (has been / had been / were)
6. You .... eat too much.
   (wouldn't / should / shouldn't)
7. You .... see if you close your eyes.
   (must / can't / can)
8. You .... go to bed if you are tired.
   (ought to / would / shouldn't)
9. You .... be kind to animals.
   (should / needn't / would)
10. .... I bring your coat?
    (shall / will / might)
11. .... we go for a walk?
    (will / shall / would)
12. This small hat .... be his because his head is very big.
    (may / can't / must)
13. You .... drive on the left in England.
    (must / mustn't / shouldn't)
14. You .... drive on the left in Spain.
    (must / mustn't / shouldn't)
15. .... you lend me a pound?
    (shall / will / should)

61

VERBOS. Escríbase una de las formas apropiadas de la combinación *There + to be* en los espacios punteados. En algunos casos, hay que añadir un *Modal Verb*.

1. .... always a policeman at this crossroads because otherwise there would be many accidents.
2. .... a table in that room, but I'm not quite sure.
3. .... an apple-tree in that park now?
4. .... still some beautiful castles.
5. .... a drunk in the street yesterday.
6. .... three thieves near the bank last night.
7. .... no cars in the street tomorrow, because it is a holiday.
8. .... no sugar in my tea!

9. .... no children in the school playground next Sunday.
10. .... a letter on that table last Monday.
11. .... a lot of things to do last week.
12. .... a lot of subjects to study next year.
13. .... somebody in that room. I can hear people talking.
14. .... anything to do?
15. .... nothing like staying at home.

62

VERBOS. Complétense las frases siguientes con verbos irregulares conjugados adecuadamente.

1. I saw Tom, but I didn't .... Tony.
2. The dog didn't bite me. It .... my brother.
3. The wind blew from the north. It didn't .... from the south.
4. Spell your name. - I've already .... it.
5. When did she come? - She .... yesterday.
6. Tell him to send the parcel. - He has already .... it.
7. Does the sun rise at six? - No, it .... at seven.
8. Did he become a lawyer? - No, he .... a teacher.
9. Where did you find the money? - I .... it in this box.
10. I usually .... at four, but yesterday I left at six.
11. Did you hear that noise? - Yes, I .... it.
12. We .... in the pool. We didn't swim in the sea.

63

VERBOS. Complétense las siguientes oraciones con el tiempo apropiado del verbo irregular, cuyo infinitivo se da entre paréntesis.

1. I .... a sandwich, because I was hungry. (eat)
2. They have .... a new flat, because they are rich. (buy)
3. She .... some water, because she was thirsty. (drink)
4. They have just .... a new bridge. (build)
5. I have just .... an interesting film. (see)
6. He has .... us a funny story. (tell)
7. The cook .... the cake with this knife. (cut)
8. I .... the vase on the table five minutes ago. (put)
9. They .... their car, because they needed money. (sell)
10. I have .... that song many times. (hear)

64

VERBOS. Colóquese, en los huecos punteados, la forma correcta del verbo irregular, que se da entre paréntesis.

1. Yesterday Tim .... a glass of milk.
   (drink / drank / drunk)
2. I often .... to the cinema.
   (go / went / gone)
3. Pamela .... a letter to her family every week.
   (writes / wrote / written)
4. He .... to read the newspaper a moment ago.
   (begin / began / begun)
5. My friend has just .... English.
   (speak / spoke / spoken)
6. He has .... me some money.
   (give / gave / given)
7. She never ....
   (sings / sang / sung)
8. Have you .... it yet?
   (do / did / done)
9. Last week I .... a very nice film.
   (see / saw / seen)
10. I haven't .... it.
    (forget / forgot / forgotten)
11. I have never .... there.
    (be / was / been)
12. The boys .... the window a moment ago.
    (break / broke / broken)
13. Peter has gone to the dentist to have a tooth .... out.
    (take / took / taken)
14. Shall we .... out tonight?
    (eat / ate / eaten)
15. Does your dog .... ?
    (bite / bit / bitten)

65

VERBOS. Elíjase la partícula apropiada para formar *Phrasal Verbs*.

1. I've decided to give .... smoking.
   (in / out / up / away / on)
2. How are you getting .... with your English?
   (out / in / away / on / up)

3. When the train went .... the rails, sixty people were injured.
   (down / off / out / away / in)
4. I'm going to look .... this word in the dictionary.
   (down / on / in / up / about)
5. Mrs Evans takes .... lodgers occasionally.
   (down / up / in / back / on)
6. I didn't go to bed at ten. I stayed .... until twelve.
   (up / in / on / down / out)
7. As it was cold, I turned .... the collar of my coat.
   (in / on / up / out / down)
8. The car broke .... on the road.
   (down / in / on / away / off)
9. Put .... your coat. It's cold today.
   (in / on / up / down / out)
10. Try this hat ....
    (down / out / in / on / away)
11. They have pulled .... the old hospital.
    (on / down / in / away / out)
12. This clock is fast. Put it ....
    (on / back / over / away / in)
13. You should turn .... the electric heater. It's very cold.
    (in / off / on / away / down)
14. We're going to set .... a business in London.
    (off / up / in / on / down)
15. He's a good friend. He'll never let me ....
    (up / away / down / on / in)

66

VERBOS. Complétense estos verbos con la partícula adecuada para formar *Phrasal Verbs*.

1. Pedir (algo): To ask ....
2. Ponerse (una prenda): To put ....
3. Quitarse (una prenda): To take ....
4. Buscar (un objeto): To look ....
5. Sacar (algo de un cajón): To take ....
6. Meter (algo en un cajón): To put ....
7. Esperar (a alguien): To wait ....
8. Pagar (algo que se compra): To pay ....
9. Entrar (en un lugar): To go ....
10. Salir (de un lugar): To go ....
11. Encender (la luz): To switch ....
12. Apagar (la luz): To switch ....

13. Devolver (algo): To give ....
14. Apagar (el fuego): To put ....
15. Recoger (del suelo): To pick ....

67

VERBOS. De cada línea, subráyense dos *Phrasal Verbs* que sean sinónimos.

1. Switch on, switch off, turn off, let off, let on.
2. Run into, come across, go across, go into, come into.
3. Fill in, fall in, fill out, fall on, feel on.
4. Walk up, walk off, walk away, walk on, walk about.
5. Put up, bring up, call up, throw up, buy up, burn up.
6. Run up, run out, run off, run into, run away.
7. Close up, catch up, call up, put up, ring up.
8. Put up, put off, put down, put back, put in.
9. Throw over, take up, make up, think over, think up.
10. Throw away, go away, come away, throw out, put out.

68

VERBOS. Elíjase el significado apropiado de cada *Phrasal Verb*.

1. Break away.
   a) irrumpir; b) soltarse; c) averiarse.
2. Cut out.
   a) recortar; b) triturar; c) acercarse.
3. Do up.
   a) alejarse; b) subir c) abrochar.
4. Carry out.
   a) gritar; b) entrar; c) llevar a cabo.
5. Go across.
   a) atravesar; b) continuar; c) marcharse.
6. Knock down.
   a) golpear; b) derribar; c) aterrizar.
7. Take off (un avión).
   a) despegar; b) aterrizar; c) llegar.
8. Write down (para no olvidar).
   a) escribir; b) anotar; c) escribir a máquina.
9. Try on (una prenda).
   a) planchar; b) ponerse; c) probarse.

10. Blow up.
    a) volar (un avión); b) volar (con un explosivo); c) resoplar.
11. Give back.
    a) devolver; b) cambiar; c) desistir.
12. Eat up.
    a) comer en casa; b) comer fuera de casa; c) comérselo todo.

69

VERBOS. Rellénense los espacios punteados, eligiendo la forma de infinitivo correcta (con o sin *to*).

1. I would like .... to Paris by car.
   (go / to go)
2. I want you .... your holidays in Málaga.
   (spend / to spend)
3. I didn't see the boys .... in the river.
   (bathe / to bathe)
4. Will you .... another cake?
   (have / to have)
5. She ought .... to the doctor's just now.
   (go / to go)
6. Did you manage .... the tickets for the theatre?
   (get / to get)
7. The girl refuses ....
   (eat / to eat)
8. I made them .... hard.
   (work / to work)
9. These pupils want .... Spanish next term.
   (learn / to learn)
10. Please tell me how .... this sentence.
    (translate / to translate)
11. I was about .... when Joan came into the room.
    (speak / to speak)
12. I have .... them today.
    (telephone / to telephone)
13. I can't .... this table. It's very heavy.
    (lift / to lift)
14. He may .... next month.
    (come / to come)
15. The teacher asked the pupils ....
    (stand up / to stand up)

70

VERBOS. Usese la partícula *to* donde sea preciso. Donde no lo sea, colóquese un aspa (X).

1. I have .... open this box.
2. The lecturer should .... speak louder.
3. Once I heard him .... sing a nice song.
4. We used .... stay at this hotel.
5. You may .... take the dog for a walk if you want to.
6. I expected you .... tell me the truth.
7. What do you want me .... do now?
8. I must .... go to work every day.
9. Try .... get up earlier.
10. I hope .... see them soon.
11. He ordered the wine .... be served at once.
12. This exercise is very easy .... do.
13. We had better .... stop working now.
14. He does nothing but .... laugh.
15. She told me not .... do it again.

71

VERBOS. Transfórmense las oraciones siguientes de forma que el infinitivo, que aparece escrito con letra cursiva, se convierta en *gerund* con oficio de sujeto, p. ej. *To read is my favourite hobby* pasa a ser: *Reading is my favourite hobby*.

1. It is interesting *to paint*.
2. It isn't easy *to spell* English words.
3. It is good exercise *to walk*.
4. It is dangerous *to drive* a car at full speed.
5. It is very difficult *to win* a price.
6. It takes a long time *to choose* presents for Christmas.
7. *To eat* is necessary for everybody.
8. *To play* the piano is marvellous.
9. *To work* hard is tiring.
10. *To learn* languages is necessary nowadays.

72

VERBOS. Conviértanse cada verbo que está entre paréntesis en *gerund* con oficio de objeto directo.

1. Please stop (talk). The teacher is looking at us.
2. You must avoid (drink) so much whisky.
3. I remember (see) that film.
4. I like (read) in bed.
5. I don't mind (work) hard.
6. I couldn't help (laugh) when I saw him.
7. The young man admitted (steal) the money.
8. I detest (go) out in the rain.
9. Jack dreads (hear) her voice.
10. I finished (write) the book last week.

73

VERBOS. Póngase el verbo que está entre paréntesis en su forma correcta de *gerund* tras preposición.

1. Jack went out without (say) good-bye.
2. I am very fond of (read) novels.
3. This pencil is for (draw).
4. He earns his living by (teach) English.
5. After (take) the medicine, he felt better.
6. Are you used to (travel) by air?
7. I can't prevent my brother from (waste) his money.
8. Before (come) into the room, knock at the door.
9. I'll study geography instead of (watch) television.
10. I'm thinking of (go) to Edinburgh soon.

74

VERBOS. Colóquense *Present Participles* en los espacios punteados, de forma que las frases tengan sentido. Utilícense los siguientes:

*writing   speaking   living   bathing   smoking
playing   having   watching   going   driving*

1. He is .... to his friend on the telephone.
2. I'm .... in Madrid now.

3. Look, there's a man .... in the river.
4. Mr Hilton is .... a pipe.
5. John is .... a letter to his parents.
6. They're .... television in the sitting-room.
7. That boy is .... along the street.
8. My friend is .... golf just now.
9. I saw Joan .... her car a moment ago.
10. Mrs Wilson is .... lunch with her family.

75

VERBOS. Subráyense las alternativas correctas en cada caso, teniendo en cuenta que, a veces, son posibles dos de ellas.

1. It began (to rain / rain / raining) at four o'clock.
2. I let the boys (to go / go / going) to the cinema.
3. I propose (to go / go / going) on holiday together.
4. The boss made us (to work / work / working) hard.
5. What are you going (to do / do / doing)?
6. He continued (to work / work / working) after lunch.
7. I'll get your brother (to paint / paint / painting) the doors again.
8. He said it started (to snow / snow / snowing) during the night.
9. I think you must not delay (to send / send / sending) the telegram.
10. What does he intend (to do / do / doing) now?
11. She promised (to stay / stay / staying) with us.
12. I hate (to scrub / scrub / scrubbing) the floors.

76

VERBOS. Subráyese la forma correcta (infinitivo -con o sin *to*- o *gerund*), según sea lo adecuado en cada caso.

1. She's fond of .... songs.
   (sing / to sing / singing)
2. I would like .... Russian.
   (speak / to speak / speaking)
3. I prefer .... rather than watch television.
   (read / to read / reading)
4. The boy denied .... the lemonade.
   (drink / to drink / drinking)
5. You must .... if you want to live.
   (eat / to eat / eating)

6. I enjoy .... museums.
   (visit / to visit / visiting)
7. Have you finished .... the novel?
   (translate / to translate / translating)
8. There is nothing like ....
   (travel / to travel / travelling)
9. Would you mind .... the door?
   (close / to close / closing)
10. I think this lesson is too difficult for us ....
    (understand / to understand / understanding)
11. You had better .... with us.
    (stay / to stay / staying)
12. It is no use .... to deceive my brother.
    (try / to try / trying)
13. I can't .... without wine for lunch.
    (do / to do / doing)
14. I hope .... you soon.
    (see / to see / seeing)
15. Can you .... the guitar?
    (play / to play / playing)

77

VERBOS. Póngase *to* donde sea necesario. Donde no lo sea, márquese con un aspa (X).

1. My parents decided .... spend their holidays in Marbella.
2. Did you see the horse .... jump over the fence?
3. He made us .... walk fast.
4. Let the children .... come with me.
5. I want .... learn how to do it.
6. I heard him .... sing at the Westminster Theatre.
7. I told him .... mend the puncture.
8. I want my daughter .... become famous.
9. I would like .... meet your parents.
10. Do you expect .... pass your exam?
11. I'm sorry, but I can't .... stop; somebody is waiting for me.
12. Please have the boys .... bring the piano to my house as soon as possible.
13. I'll get the girl .... sweep the floor.
14. Must you .... go just now?
15. Your had better .... take this medicine.
16. You ought .... obey your parents.
17. He was made .... work hard.

18. You are asked .... answer all these questions.
19. He asked me .... open the door.
20. I would rather .... stay at home than go abroad.

78

VERBOS. Escríbanse estas oraciones en voz pasiva, teniendo en cuenta que el objeto directo de la oración en activa (en cursiva) debe aparecer como sujeto de la oración pasiva, y que no es necesario especificar el agente, p. ej. *They / Somebody found the money* pasa a ser: *The money was found.*

1. They are painting *the classroom*.
2. They found *the lost child*.
3. Somebody has stolen *my dictionary*.
4. Somebody will type *the letters*.
5. They rescued *Mr Wilson*.
6. Somebody should wash *the dishes*.
7. Somebody must change *the wheel*.
8. They lowered *the rope*.
9. They sent *the parcels* to Spain.

79

VERBOS. Cámbiense las oraciones siguientes a voz pasiva, teniendo en cuenta que el objeto indirecto, que aparece en cursiva, se convierte en sujeto, p. ej. *They gave me a present* pasa a ser: *I was given a present.*

1. They promised *me* a new job.
2. They showed *her* some nice ties.
3. They asked *him* three questions.
4. They taught *her* how to play the piano.
5. They offered *me* a cup of tea.
6. They told *them* the results of the exam.
7. They gave *me* a watch as a present.
8. They paid *Pat* the money he had earned.
9. They asked *me* to leave.
10. They made *us* work hard.
11. They told *you* to speak more slowly.
12. They advised *me* to be silent.

80

VERBOS. Complétense las oraciones con la forma y el tiempo correcto de *use, used to* o *be used to*, según el caso.

1. What are you going to .... that paint for?
2. I .... play football, but I don't anymore.
3. He .... staying up so late during the week.
4. Scissors .... for cutting.
5. It was strange to live in New York at first but we soon got .... to it.
6. There never .... to be so much traffic.
7. .... you .... to live next door to Joan?
8. There .... be fewer people travelling by air.
9. Where .... he .... to play tennis?
10. You can have this jersey. I won't .... it again.
11. We .... go to the theatre until we moved to the town centre. Now we go every month.
12. I didn't enjoy living in Paris in the beginning as I .... hearing a foreign language all day.
13. She's rich. She .... having a lot of money. She .... being poor.
14. We .... live in a very small flat, then we moved into a house. We're still .... having so much space.
15. What games did you .... play when you were a child?
16. There are still three museums in the city but there .... be many more.
17. Are you .... eating Chinese food? Can you .... chopsticks?
18. He doesn't play rugby now but he ....
19. Where did she .... live?

81

VERBOS. Este ejercicio trata del verbo *to have* en el sentido llamado en inglés *causative*. Con esta función se emplea para describir acciones que uno no hace por sí solo, sino que las manda hacer, p. ej. *Mrs Baker doesn't cut her own hair. She has it cut by the hair-dresser* (hace que se lo corte el peluquero).

1. Mr Jones didn't repair the car himself. He .... at the garage.
2. We won't install the computer ourselves. We'll .... by the manufacturer.
3. Mr Jones never types letters. He .... by a secretary.
4. Jane doesn't press her husband's shirts. She .... at the cleaner's.

5. Martin's mother didn't make the birthday cake for the party. She .... by a catering company.
6. She didn't pay her bills personally. She .... by bank transfer.
7. We don't clean delicate upholstery here. We .... professionally.
8. In a hotel, guests don't normally make their own beds. They .... by a chambermaid.
9. He doesn't make his own suits. He .... by a tailor in town.
10. Patients don't test their own eyesight. They .... by an optician.
11. Did you check the oil level in your car? No I .... at the garage
12. And did you repair the flat tyres? No .... at the garage, too.

82

VERBOS. Complétense las oraciones siguientes con la forma y el tiempo apropiado de los verbos *Make* y *Do,* según sea el caso.

1. Do you know how to .... a cake?
2. Jim hasn't .... his bed this morning.
3. Ask Mr Brown what he .... for a living.
4. Those children are .... their homework.
5. .... your shoes up!
6. What a noise those boys are ....!
7. I didn't .... any spelling mistakes in my essay.
8. Mary is .... very well at school.
9. I'm sure you can .... better than that!
10. You should always .... your best.
11. .... sure you're on time for the lesson.
12. He always .... his work well at school last year.
13. Would you .... me a favour?
14. They shouldn't .... promises they can't keep.
15. Who is going to .... the washing up?

83

ADVERBIOS. Vuélvase a escribir cada oración, colocando el adverbio de tiempo, que se presenta entre paréntesis, en su lugar correspondiente.

1. He reads in bed (never).
2. I write with my father's pen (seldom).
3. He is ready to tell them stories (always).
4. The girl doesn't help her mother (always).

5. His hands are dirty (often).
6. You aren't ready (usually).
7. I go to the cinema in the evening (sometimes).
8. Does she cook lunch? (usually).
9. They come in the morning (generally).
10. My cousin came two hours (ago).
11. Philip has broken the vase (just).
12. Have you been to London? (ever).
13. She has come in the morning (never).
14. Betty drinks milk (sometimes).
15. I have seen that programme (already).
16. Has she arrived? (yet).
17. They are asleep (still).
18. Did she ask for their help? (ever).
19. I haven't had breakfast (yet).
20. My parents go to the theatre in the evening (often).

84

ADVERBIOS. Elíjase el adverbio adecuado y escríbase en cada uno de los espacios punteados.

1. The sun .... rises in the east.
   a) always; b) never; c) sometimes.
2. Summer in Edinburgh is .... hot.
   a) always; b) seldom; c) usually.
3. A tortoise .... walks slowly.
   a) always; b) seldom; c) sometimes.
4. We .... have breakfast in the afternoon.
   a) always; b) never; c) often.
5. It .... rains in Vigo.
   a) always; b) never; c) usually.
6. I .... go to the cinema because I don't like it.
   a) always; b) never; c) usually.
7. The boy is eating .... because he is in a hurry.
   a) quickly; b) slowly; c) carefully.
8. Speak .... I can't understand you.
   a) quickly; b) clearly; c) fast.
9. This man walks .... because he's very old.
   a) quickly; b) slowly; c) fast.
10. He's .... late. He's always punctual.
    a) never; b) always; c) often.

85

ADVERBIOS. Introdúzcase en estas frases el elemento adverbial de tiempo, lugar o modo, propuesto entre paréntesis, en cada caso.

1. I had forgotten the time (completely).
2. She smokes (too much).
3. The lift operates (automatically).
4. The secretary opens the mail (in the morning).
5. We read that magazine (every week).
6. She telephones me (in the afternoon).
7. This book is interesting (extremely).
8. He will return the dictionary (next week).
9. Betty is tired (easily).
10. The work was done (badly).

86

ADVERBIOS. Escríbanse estas oraciones, introduciendo los adverbios de modo, que están entre paréntesis.

1. He invited me to the theatre (timidly).
2. The man said that it wasn't a joke (sarcastically).
3. We requested him to send the letter at once (emphatically).
4. She told the boy to eat his dinner (insistently).
5. That boy observed that it wasn't a common bird (shrewdly).
6. She answered what she thought at that moment (wisely).
7. She asked them to stay with her (politely).
8. I explained to them how to do the test (carefully).
9. Your brother ordered me to open the door (rudely).
10. Joan told us that she could speak three languages (boastfully).

87

ADVERBIOS. En este ejercicio se han de terminar las oraciones, colocando los elementos adverbiales de tiempo, lugar o modo en el orden adecuado.

1. He found the knife..............
   (yesterday / in a drawer)
2. I met Pamela..............
   (this month / in one of my classes)
3. The teacher explained the lessons..............
   (in class / last week)

4. She drove her car............
   (last night / very fast)
5. He speaks English............
   (now / very well)
6. Tim is a student............
   (this year / at university)
7. That film was shown............
   (at the Capitol / last month)
8. He went............
   (there / once)
9. They sang............
   (very well / last night)
10. Read the letter............
    (now / slowly)

88

ADVERBIOS. Escríbanse estas oraciones, introduciendo la frase adverbial que se propone en cada caso.

1. They ate all the cakes yesterday.
   (at the party)
2. Johnny painted this picture a week ago.
   (very carefully)
3. The little girl drew the tree very well.
   (in class)
4. Andrew goes to school in the morning.
   (by bus)
5. Elizabeth ironed my trousers very well.
   (a week ago)
6. The fat man ate a lot of sandwiches.
   (at the party)
7. I bought this tie cheaply.
   (last Wednesday)
8. The children play football in the park.
   (in summer)
9. She cooks dinner at seven o'clock.
   (in the kitchen)

89

ADVERBIOS. Termínense estas oraciones colocando al final los adverbios de modo y lugar, entre paréntesis, en el orden adecuado.

1. I type letters ....
   (in the office / carefully)
2. They walked ....
   (along the street / slowly)
3. The girl spoke English ....
   (fluently / in class)
4. James drives ....
   (along the road / fast)
5. These students study geography ....
   (on Mondays / reluctantly)
6. The manager dictated the letter ....
   (quickly / in his office)
7. He fought ....
   (in the war / bravely)
8. Those boys play ....
   (noisily / in the park)
9. She answered all the questions ....
   (politely / at the meeting)
10. The woman ironed my shirt ....
    (very well / on that table)

90

ADVERBIOS. Complétense estas frases colocando al final los elementos adverbiales de modo y tiempo, en el orden correcto.

1. We considered the matter ....
   (very carefully / yesterday)
2. I shall drive to the station ....
   (this afternoon / very slowly)
3. She spoke ....
   (last night / frankly)
4. James answered my questions ....
   (calmly / a week ago)
5. The teacher explained the lesson ....
   (a month ago / clearly)
6. My father works ....
   (from Monday to Friday / tirelessly)

7. He pronounced these words ....
   (distinctly / last Sunday)
8. Pete studied philosophy ....
   (last year / enthusiastically)
9. His aunt sings ....
   (nicely / every day)
10. Andrew did his exercises ....
    (quickly / on Friday)

91

ADVERBIOS. Complétense estas frases, colocando al final los elementos adverbiales de tiempo y lugar, en el orden adecuado.

1. I saw your grandfather ....
   (in the street / on Tuesday)
2. Her father worked ....
   (last year / at that factory)
3. My parents walk ....
   (in the park / on Sundays)
4. I have dinner ....
   (every day / at a restaurant)
5. I was ....
   (last week / in London)
6. Pete is going to stay ....
   (tomorrow / in a hotel)
7. He hung the picture ....
   (on that wall / a week ago)
8. Miss Smith typed that letter ....
   (in the office / this morning)
9. The children are going to play ....
   (this afternoon / in this room)
10. Mr Carter spoke ....
    (here / yesterday)

92

ADVERBIOS. Termínense estas frases, colocando al final los elementos adverbiales de modo, lugar y tiempo en el orden apropiado.

1. Mary walks ....
   (slowly / in the park / in the afternoons)

2. The little girl plays ....
   (very happily / here / every day)
3. The manager spoke ....
   (very emphatically / last week / at the meeting)
4. That teacher asks questions ....
   (very quickly / in class / every day)
5. Please type my report ....
   (at once / in your office / very carefully)
6. You didn't eat your cake ....
   (yesterday / quietly / in the playground)
7. Will you be able to explain the lesson .... ?
   (in class / tomorrow / slowly)
8. They're talking ....
   (very noisily / in that room / at this moment)
9. The teacher speaks ....
   (on Tuesdays / slowly / in the beginners' class)

93

ADVERBIOS. Formúlese una pregunta con el adverbio interrogativo apropiado, de acuerdo con las palabras en cursiva de cada respuesta.

1. ....? - They live *in Paris*.
2. ....? - I wrote it *yesterday*.
3. ....? - She came *by bus*.
4. ....? - They ran *because they were late*.
5. ....? - I hit the thief *on the head*.
6. ....? - I've come *because I want to see you*.
7. ....? - I'm *very well*, thank you.
8. ....? - He will come *tomorrow*.
9. ....? - She went *to India*.
10. ....? - He's learning English *because he wants to go to London*.

94

ADVERBIOS. Tradúzcanse al inglés estas frases, prestando especial atención a los adverbios, que se dan en cursiva.

1. Yo leo *más deprisa* que Bruce.
2. Tony es el chico que corre *más deprisa*.
3. Este coche no es *suficientemente* grande para nosotros.
4. Tengo *solamente* ochenta libras.
5. El té está *demasiado* caliente.
6. El autobús estaba *totalmente* lleno.

7. Este es el mejor vino que *jamás* he bebido.
8. Yo *también* tengo coche.
9. Como médico es *bastante* bueno.
10. ¿Quieres algo *más*?
11. Este sombrero es *demasiado* grande para mí.
12. Si trabajas *mucho*, ganarás más dinero.
13. Me gustan *mucho* las manzanas.
14. Dos libras es *demasiado* por este bolígrafo.
15. El no va, ni yo *tampoco* voy.
16. Tony habla *muy mal* el español.
17. El *apenas* sabe escribir.
18. Este perfume huele *bien*.

95

ADVERBIOS. Colóquese en cada oración los adverbios que faltan, y que se han de elegir de entre los siguientes:

since   now   ago   yet   still   already

1. Have you done your homework ....? - No, not ....
2. The last accident at the factory happened 20 years .... There hasn't been another one ....
3. I'm typing your letters .... I .... haven't finished them.
4. The flight to London left 20 minutes ...., but the plane to Rome hasn't taken off .... It's .... on the ground.
5. Mr Williams hasn't left the office .... in fact, I'm talking to him right ....
6. You .... haven't received my letter? But I sent it 5 days ....!
7. Is Bill .... at school? - No he's .... on his way home. He left 10 minutes ....

96

ADVERBIOS / ADJETIVOS. Colóquense los adverbios y adjetivos, que aparecen entre paréntesis, en sus lugares correspondientes para que las oraciones siguientes tengan sentido.

1. He is a .... student. He translates his exercises ....
   (clever / cleverly)
2. The maid ironed the shirts .... She is always very .... in her work.
   (careful / carefully)

3. Jane is a .... typist. She types ....
   (well / good)
4. He listened very ...., although he's not a .... man!
   (patient / patiently)
5. She's .... in French. She speaks it ....
   (fluently / fluent)
6. His memory is not very .... He doesn't remember names, numbers or faces ....
   (well / good)
7. She did .... in the test and got .... marks.
   (well / good)
8. He's a .... driver; he drives ....
   (dangerous / dangerously)

97

ADVERBIOS / ADJETIVOS. En este ejercicio se contrasta *too* con *enough*. Colóquese la palabra que falta en cada caso.

1. I haven't got .... money for a new car.
2. She won't buy the dress. It's .... expensive.
3. He won't drink coffee if it's .... strong or if it doesn't have .... sugar in it.
4. You're not old .... to drive. You're only 15!
5. He forgot to post the letter and now it's .... late.
6. They said he didn't have .... experience to work as a pilot.
7. They said he wasn't reliable .... to work at the factory.
8. After the accident the newspaper reported that the train driver hadn't been experienced ....
9. I can make some more coffee if there isn't ....
10. My mother says this weather is .... hot for her!
11. This box is .... heavy. I'm not strong .... to lift it!
12. The bridge is high .... for a car to go under, but .... low for a bus.
13. Is the radio loud .... for you? Oh, it's .... loud, is it? Sorry.
14. Shall we go out for dinner or is it .... late now?
15. He says he doesn't feel well .... to go to school today.

98

ADVERBIOS / ADJETIVOS. En este ejercicio se contrasta *so* con *such*. Colóquese una de las dos palabras en cada frase.

1. I've never seen .... a pretty dress!
2. It was .... a difficult exam that many students failed.

3. The restaurant was .... expensive that we won't be going there again. And it was .... a bad meal, too!
4. We had .... bad weather in London that we couldn't do much sightseeing. It was .... cold that we had to wear our coats every day.
5. I've got .... a lot of work to do!
6. We're having .... a busy time in the shop! Everyone is doing their Christmas shopping.
7. The car park was .... full that we had to leave the car outside in the street.
8. The explosion was .... loud that it could be heard a mile away.
9. It was .... an interesting book that he couldn't put it down.
10. These are .... comfortable shoes that I wear them everywhere.
11. Taxis are .... expensive these days!

99

PREPOSICIONES. Colóquese *to* o *for*, según el sentido de la frase.

1. He is studying hard .... an examination.
2. The boy threw the ball .... me.
3. Thank you .... coming.
4. We invited Bruce .... our house for dinner.
5. That sounds very suspicious .... me.
6. It is too cold .... us to live here.
7. Are you staying after class .... the lecture?
8. It's 50 miles .... Paris.
9. I waited half an hour .... the bus.
10. Joan is always kind .... animals.

100

PREPOSICIONES. Elíjase entre las preposiciones *at* o *in* y escríbase una de ellas en cada espacio punteado.

1. There is a garden .... the front of the house.
2. There is a hole .... in my trousers.
3. The hole is .... the bottom of the leg near the turnup.
4. Mr Miller is .... front of the house.
5. There is a kitchen .... the back of the house.
6. Mr Evans spoke .... a loud voice.
7. I'm interested .... music.
8. There is a horse .... the foreground of the picture.
9. There is a garden .... the back of the house.

10. Can you see a kennel .... the side of the house?

101

PREPOSICIONES. Colóquese *for* o *during*, según el caso.

1. It snowed .... the afternoon.
2. I was in London .... a week.
3. I have been here .... two hours.
4. She came .... my absence.
5. It rained .... an hour yesterday.
6. The sun shines .... the day.
7. Pamela was in Paris .... a long time.
8. She always reads .... half an hour before going to bed.
9. The moon shines .... the night.
10. I've been living in Madrid .... ten years.

102

PREPOSICIONES. Escríbase *between* o *among*, según sea necesario.

1. The eternal war .... men and women.
2. I am sitting .... Tim and Tom.
3. We are .... friends.
4. Madrid is .... the largest cities in the world.
5. He found the letter .... his papers.
6. I always read .... the lines.
7. He'll divide the money .... the five of you.
8. There is a good road .... Madrid and Toledo.
9. We shall arrive .... four and five o'clock.
10. There was a great war .... several European nations.

103

PREPOSICIONES. Complétense estas frases con *for* o *since*.

1. Pam and Peggy have been waiting here .... three hours.
2. Mr Carter has worked .... seven o'clock.
3. We haven't seen them .... 1998.
4. She hasn't drunk tea .... a week.
5. They have not been here .... last week.
6. You have studied French .... two years.
7. We have lived in Barcelona .... August.

8. Those boys have played football .... two hours.
9. Mrs Grey hasn't seen her daughter .... last year.
10. She has listened to the radio .... an hour.
11. We haven't visited our grandfather .... last summer.
12. Jack has been writing letters .... two days.

104

PREPOSICIONES. Complétense estas frases con *of* o *from*.

1. Their method is different .... ours.
2. Nobody is free .... error.
3. I feel suspicious .... Bruce.
4. I would like to live in a house remote .... any town.
5. The explorer was unaware .... the danger.
6. He is very proud .... his work.
7. I must say that the man is innocent .... the charge.
8. They've just returned .... the expedition.
9. My hands smell .... soap.
10. I bought this novel .... the bookseller's.

105

PREPOSICIONES. Complétense estas oraciones con *on* o *in*.

1. He talked .... a loud voice.
2. They live .... the continent, don't they?
3. Write it .... the blackboard, please.
4. He is a man .... his fifties.
5. She has a ring .... her finger.
6. I work .... a farm.
7. You are always .... the way.
8. I met him .... my way home.
9. The man .... the black hat is a detective.
10. They'll come home .... New Year's day.

106

PREPOSICIONES. Elíjase entre las preposiciones *in, into* o *to* para completar estas frases.

1. The boy jumped .... the river.
2. Come .... please.
3. Come .... the room and sit down.
4. My mother poured the milk .... the jug.

5. There's a lion .... that cage.
6. There are some very high buildings .... Madrid.
7. I go .... the supermarket every day.
8. After her illness, my sister returned .... work.
9. The ambassador walked .... the next hall, where the minister was waiting.
10. My father is .... his office at this moment.

107

PREPOSICIONES. Colóquese una de las preposiciones *at, on* o *in* en cada espacio punteado.

1. Mr Lodge is .... the United States.
2. He is studying French .... university.
3. He always arrives .... school a little late.
4. There's a good shop .... the corner.
5. She's lying .... bed.
6. The postman is .... the door.
7. He was wounded .... the leg.
8. I was annoyed .... her mistakes.
9. I have no interest .... this matter.
10. Write your name .... the end of the letter.

108

PREPOSICIONES. Escójase la preposición correcta entre las tres que se proponen en cada caso.

1. He went .... the street.
   (along / by / through)
2. I want to stay .... home.
   (at / by / to)
3. They arrived .... four o'clock.
   (in / to / at)
4. My brother came home .... March 2nd.
   (at / on / in)
5. Joe always travels .... train.
   (in / on / by)
6. We often go for a walk .... the park.
   (by / in / through)
7. She waited .... the bus.
   (to / for / at)

8. There is a test .... the next page.
   (in / on / at)
9. There was a policeman .... the crossroads.
   (in / at / on)
10. We have no money .... this moment.
    (in / at / on)

109

PREPOSICIONES. Escríbase en estas frases la preposición adecuada. Escójase entre las siguientes:

along   on   for   by   into   in

1. Mr Grey prefers tea .... breakfast.
2. Pat goes to work .... train.
3. He is going .... the room.
4. Go straight .... this road, then turn left.
5. I have a watch .... my wrist.
6. The church is .... the right.
7. This symphony was composed .... Beethoven.
8. He went there .... the seventh of May.
9. I went for a walk .... the park.
10. Mr Armstrong gave a lecture .... philosophy.

110

PREPOSICIONES. Elíjase la preposición adecuada.

at   between   on   with   from   for   to

1. She lives .... Mr and Mrs Carter.
2. I am studying .... Madrid University.
3. He notices the differences .... British and Spanish customs.
4. We are going to the country .... vacation.
5. You receive many letters .... your friends.
6. I've been listening to the radio .... an hour.
7. There was a good film .... the Capitol last week.
8. They invited us .... dinner.
9. He rented the house .... fifty pounds a month.
10. I am studying English .... pleasure.

111
PREPOSICIONES. Escójase la preposición correcta.

1. What's the matter (with / to / at) you?
2. I have a pain (on / in / at) my stomach.
3. I like listening (at / on / to) her.
4. Let's wait (for / at / to) the bus.
5. I'm getting off (on / at / in) the next stop.
6. Let's walk (at / to / in) the bus-stop.
7. The test consists (on / of / at) twenty simple questions.
8. Have you brought your dictionary (with / on / to) you?
9. I don't like the idea (for / on / of) going to Paris.
10. I can't read (without / from / on) glasses.

112
PREPOSICIONES. Escójase la preposición correcta.

for   to   in   at   on

1. There were many people .... the meeting.
2. You were late .... class this morning.
3. She likes hamburgers .... lunch.
4. We made a good impression .... them.
5. He is going to call .... you this morning.
6. He is working .... his thesis.
7. I heard the news broadcast .... noon.
8. There were many people .... the park today.
9. Have you ever been .... South America?
10. I usually go home .... lunch.

113
PREPOSICIONES. Elíjase la preposición adecuada.

of   at   to   for   from   on

1. I always watch television .... night.
2. Did she talk .... you?
3. My cousin Philip always comes .... Mondays.
4. Where are you ....?
5. I'm looking .... the book I lost.

6. We usually have breakfast .... eight o'clock in the morning.
7. He listens .... the radio in the evening.
8. What are you looking ....? I'm looking at these flowers.
9. I'm thinking .... going to Paris to visit my friends.
10. She often has tea instead .... coffee.

114

PREPOSICIONES. Rellénense los espacios punteados con la preposición que corresponda.

in at for with from for of to

1. The foreman spoke .... me.
2. Which is the coldest country .... the world?
3. The shop-assistant said, "What can I do .... you?"
4. Is your farm far .... here?
5. The teacher was angry .... us.
6. I like eggs .... breakfast.
7. The child always cries .... night.
8. What is she laughing ....?
9. What hotel did you stay ....?
10. I'll be there .... an hour.
11. My brother always gets up at six o'clock .... the morning.
12. My grandparents like staying .... home when it is very cold.

115

PREPOSICIONES. Colóquense dos preposiciones en cada oración. Elíjanse de entre las siguientes:

at in on over

1. Don't sit .... that sofa. Sit .... this armchair.
2. Is he .... the concert? - No, I think he is .... the cinema.
3. The plane flew .... Spain and soon arrived .... England.
4. Put these books .... that shelf and those ball-pens .... this box.
5. The picture was hanging .... the wall .... the fireplace.
6. I was .... church last Sunday when the plane flew .... the town.
7. I don't feel as happy .... this house as .... home.
8. The tea is .... the cup which is .... the saucer.

9. I shall arrive .... his house .... two o'clock.
10. If I laugh .... him he will shout .... me.

116

PREPOSICIONES. Complétese cada una de estas frases con tres preposiciones.

1. My family went .... Paris .... London .... train.
2. I made a profit .... 250 pounds .... the sale .... my car.
3. We are delighted .... the idea .... going .... Rome.
4. My sister will come back home .... eight o'clock .... the 25th .... December.
5. My father said .... me, "Beware .... judging .... appearances."
6. You must answer .... Mr Roberts .... what you did .... Monday.
7. They announced the arrival .... the plane .... the people .... the airport.
8. The radio set they were listening .... belonged .... the owner .... the house.
9. He was sitting .... his desk, drawing a horse .... a piece .... paper.
10. My father is speaking .... Mr Evans .... the pictures he has .... his office.

117

PREPOSICIONES. Escríbase la preposición apropiada al final de las siguientes preguntas.

1. What is he interested ....?
2. Who are they talking ....?
3. Who do these gloves belong ....?
4. What are you looking ....?
5. What does it depend ....?
6. What is the film ....?
7. What are you afraid ....?
8. Where does he come ....?
9. Which house does John live ....?
10. What do you want this ....?

118

PREPOSICIONES. Escríbase la preposición adecuada al final de cada una de estas oraciones de relativo.

1. This is the key I opened the door ....
2. This is the house he lives ....
3. France is the country Monique comes ....
4. Is that the treasure you dreamt ....?
5. Are those the nurses you talked ....?
6. That isn't the film I was talking ....
7. This isn't the hotel we stayed ....
8. These are the glasses we drank ....
9. That is the room the boys play ....
10. This is the ball the boys play ....
11. Rio is the place I want to go ....
12. You are the person I believe ....
13. Grass is what cows live ....
14. This bench was the one they were sitting ....

119

PREPOSICIONES. Tradúzcanse las siguientes oraciones al inglés, prestando especial atención a las preposiciones, que aparecen señaladas en cursiva.

1. El profesor dijo, "Escribid una composición *sobre* lo que queráis."
2. El chico iba *por* la calle cuando empezó a llover.
3. Este libro fue escrito *por* mi padre.
4. Esto es diferente *de* la seda.
5. Lo hicimos *en* broma.
6. Lo compré *por* diez libras.
7. Estoy avergonzado *de* ti.
8. Estoy cansado *de* trabajar.
9. Hay una mosca *en* el techo.
10. Este es el único cine *de* la ciudad.

120

CONJUNCIONES. Escójase el elemento conjuntivo correcto:

what   that   where   when   and   whether

1. You must write .... thank him.
2. The question is .... we need it or not.
3. That's not .... I expected him to say.
4. The fact is .... we're lost.
5. I'm not certain .... she lives.
6. The news .... Jean's grandmother had died took me by surprise.
7. It's very important .... they never see each other again.
8. It seems .... she had never been to England before.
9. It's very confusing .... you do not understand the language.
10. I know .... I must do.
11. You'll do this .... you like it or not.
12. Please come .... see me.

121

CONJUNCIONES. Elíjase la conjunción o palabra con valor conjuntivo apropiada en cada caso.

1. Speak more slowly so (that / how) I can understand you.
2. The shoes were (as / so) expensive that I didn't buy them.
3. (How / When) she entered the room, she sat down.
4. My brother is unhappy (because / though) he has failed.
5. (Whether / Although) he was an honest boy, nobody liked him.
6. This shows (what / that) Barbara did not tell us the truth.
7. He will go (whether / if) you ask him.
8. The dog ran so fast (as / that) he caught the rabbit.
9. Please wait here (till / because) I come back.
10. (As / How) I was in a hurry, I went by taxi.

122

CONJUNCIONES. Con cada dos oraciones, constrúyase una tercera en la que se use el elemento conjuntivo propuesto entre paréntesis.

1. I know a girl. She has two brothers. (who)
2. There isn't much water. We can't wash. (so)
3. I've brought these two cases. Charles couldn't carry them all. (because)

4. We sell books. We sell magazines. (and)
5. I arrived at the station. The train had left. (when)
6. I was tired. I didn't stop walking. (though)
7. You can't do it. I can't do it. (neither / nor)
8. I bought a cap in London. It is a very nice cap. (that)
9. I was in a hurry. I caught a plane. (as)
10. I wanted something. He gave it to me. (what)

123

CONJUNCIONES. Tradúzcanse al inglés las siguientes oraciones, prestando atención a las conjunciones (en letra cursiva).

1. ¿Quieres contestar el teléfono, *ya que* tú eres el que estás más cerca?
2. Yo enseñé a David *y* David enseñó a Tony.
3. No tiene mucho dinero, *pero* tiene muchos amigos.
4. Ponte el abrigo *si* tienes frío.
5. *Ni* tú *ni* yo podemos hacerlo.
6. No sabemos *si* está correcto o no.
7. John dice *que* tiene mucho dinero.
8. *Aunque* hice el trabajo con mucho cuidado, a ella no le gustó el resultado.
9. Pronuncia esta palabra *como* te han enseñado.
10. La chica nos miró *como si* nos entendiera.

124

CONJUNCIONES. Escójase el elemento conjuntivo que mejor complete la frase.

*after   before   if   although   unless   so that
because   as   where   when*

1. The money will be .... you left it.
2. My brother spent all the money .... I told him not to.
3. They'll see it .... they arrive. They'll be here soon.
4. He'll go home .... he has finished his homework.
5. I'd like to see them .... they go.
6. I'll close the window .... you won't catch cold.
7. You can't buy anything .... you have money.
8. I cannot stop now .... I'm in a hurry.
9. The boy pronounced the word .... he'd been taught.

10. I found the umbrella .... you had left it.
11. You can't use the underground .... you have a ticket.
12. Let me know .... you expect to be late.
13. He lives simply .... they say he's very rich.
14. .... it's raining, they'll still play football.

125

GENITIVO SAJON. Con cada dos oraciones, constrúyase una tercera que lleve el genitivo sajón, como en este modelo: *This is John. This is his car.* **Pasa a ser:** *This is John's car.*

1. This is the teacher. This is his book.
2. That is Mary. That is her bag.
3. Those are the students. Those are their books.
4. This is my friend. This is his umbrella.
5. That is your sister. That is her hat.
6. These are your brothers. These are their coins.
7. Those are the waiters. That is their money.
8. These are my children. Those are their ball-pens.
9. That is the waiter. That is his money.
10. That is the bell-boy. This is his uniform.

126

GENITIVO SAJON. Tradúzcanse al inglés las frases siguientes, prestando atención al llamado "genitivo sajón" (caso posesivo).

1. Los amigos *de Jane* y los *de Betty*.
2. Los amigos *de Jane y Betty*.
3. ¿Has estado alguna vez en la iglesia *de San Marcos*?
4. Hoy vamos a la casa *de mi hermano*.
5. La pata *de la mesa*.
6. La honradez *de los pobres*.
7. Esta es la ropa *de los chicos* que están jugando al fútbol.
8. Soy un amigo *de Jack*.
9. Este coche es *de Philip*.
10. ¿De quién es este coche? -Es *de Tony*.

127 ORDEN DE LAS PALABRAS. Escríbase en los espacios punteados una frase contruida con las palabras que se dan entre paréntesis.

1. John is from Canada. ....
   (Mary - so - is)
2. I speak English. ....
   (so - I - do)
3. I can dance. ....
   (can - they - so)
4. They didn't speak to Mr Finch yesterday. ....
   (did - we - neither)
5. My teacher speaks English. ....
   (so - my father - does)
6. I'm not a doctor. ....
   (neither - he - is)
7. He didn't see Dorothy. ....
   (I - either - didn't)
8. She couldn't come last night. ....
   (he - couldn't - either)
9. They don't live in London. ....
   (my parents - neither - do)
10. We haven't got a car. ....
    (neither - we - have)

---

128 ORDEN DE LAS PALABRAS. Reháganse estas oraciones, añadiendo las palabras que se proponen, en cada caso, entre paréntesis.

1. The car is on sale. (blue)
2. The man is a driver. (French, with the grey hair)
3. Mr Grey has read books. (a lot of, on phonetics)
4. The girl is from Germany. (who has the yellow dress on)
5. The boy who is talking to Pam is Jim's friend. (in the red sweater)
6. Please find a taxi. (my mother)
7. The men are policemen. (wearing blue uniforms)
8. Philip is in a hurry. (because he never gets up on time, always)
9. He reads the paper. (often, in the morning)
10. He has been to Belgium. (before, never)
11. I want to buy a table. (good, antique)

12. Betty is a girl. (young, pretty)

129

ORDEN DE LAS PALABRAS. Termínense estas frases con los elementos que se indican entre paréntesis en cada caso.

1. I want to know ....
   (Arthur / is / where)
2. Can you tell me ....?
   (time / what / is / it)
3. Near the park ....
   (an / old / was / house)
4. On top of the cupboard ....
   (box / a / is)
5. She wants to know ....
   (he / is / what / doing)
6. Tell me ....
   (how / it / you / did)
7. Post ....
   (letter / me / for / this)
8. Please find ....
   (a chair / Wendy / for)
9. Please find ....
   (a chair / Wendy)
10. I explained ....
    (to / lesson / the / them)

130

ORDEN DE LAS PALABRAS. Escríbanse estas frases, añadiendo los adverbios propuestos.

1. He spoke Russian.
   (very well)
2. She flew to London.
   (on the morning plane)
3. You must tighten the rope.
   (firmly)
4. I've been there.
   (never)
5. The letter was written.
   (badly)

6. His work was done.
   (carefully)
7. She speaks English.
   (badly)
8. I go there.
   (sometimes)
9. You must say that.
   (never)
10. I understand you.
    (quite)

131

ORDEN DE LAS PALABRAS. Tradúzcanse estas frases, prestando atención a las palabras escritas en cursiva.

1. Toledo es una ciudad *famosa* por su catedral.
2. Hay un chico *enfermo* en aquella cama.
3. El chico está *enfermo* hoy.
4. Necesitamos a alguien *inteligente*.
5. Tiñó el vestido de *rojo*.
6. Encontré a mi padre *herido*.
7. Una alfombra *grande de seda*.
8. Una bolsa *blanca de plástico*.
9. Un *gran* barco *antiguo inglés*.
10. Un *viejo* vestido *amarillo*.

132

ORDEN DE LAS PALABRAS. Ordénese cada grupo de palabras que se propone a continuación para construir una frase, p. ej. *(don't / beer / I / drink / usually)* **pasa a ser:** *I don't usually drink beer.*

1. (very / mother / much / play / liked / the / my)
2. (wrote / he / letters / quickly / all)
3. (ever / newspaper / he / a / hardly / reads)
4. (remembers / birthday / she / my / never)
5. (at / I / five / usually / o'clock / finish)
6. (we'll / year / go / to / probably / next / France)
7. (always / late? / you / why / are)
8. (the / to / go / they / rarely / cinema)
9. (London / it / in / rains / often)

10. (plays / father / Sundays / tennis / only / on / my)

133

ORDEN DE LAS PALABRAS. Complétense las respuestas, de acuerdo con las preguntas que se formulan, prestado especial atención a la colocación del sujeto de la oración subordinada; p.ej. *Where is Tim?* **pasa a ser:** *I don't know where Tim is.*

1. Who's that man?
   I don't know who..............................

2. What's this?
   I don't know what ....

3. Why was he absent last Monday?
   I don't know why..............................

4. What are the boys doing?
   I don't know what...........................

5. Where are they?
   I don't know where ....

134

ORDEN DE LAS PALABRAS. Escríbase cada frase, colocando los dos objetos: directo / indirecto (entre paréntesis), en el orden correcto, teniendo en cuenta que en varios casos son correctas dos posibilidades. Usese *to* **o** *for* **cuando sea necesario. P. ej.** *Sally reported (the police) (the man)* **pasa a ser:** *Sally reported the man to the police.*

1. John said (goodbye) (me).
2. I told (a story) (the children)
3. She showed (them) (it).
4. She made (a sandwich) (Peter).
5. The shopkeeper sold (a jersey) (me).
6. The shopkeeper sold (an old woman) (a jersey).
7. I promised (a reward) (whoever could find my dog).
8. Mr Wilson taught (English) (us).

135

ORDEN DE LAS PALABRAS. Vuélvanse a escribir estas oraciones, colocando la forma verbal *is* (que falta) en su lugar apropiado para que tengan sentido.

1. I'd like to know what the time by the clock in the sitting-room.
2. I want to know what your name.
3. Jack wants to know what the time.
4. Let's ask that policeman where the park.
5. Please tell me where the railway station.
6. Please tell me, where the railway station?
7. How far London from here?
8. Do you know how far London from here?
9. How old your aunt Joan?
10. I wonder how old your aunt Joan.

136

ORDEN DE LAS PALABRAS. Vuélvanse a escribir estas frases, colocando, en el orden correcto, los adjetivos que aparecen entre paréntesis.

1. Molly has a (yellow / new) dress.
2. The book is in that (plastic / blue) bag.
3. There is a (square / small) table in that corner.
4. This is a (nice / silk) handkerchief.
5. My father has bought this (Chinese / antique) vase.
6. There was a (fat / French) boy at the party.
7. Tom was carrying a (brown / big) case.
8. I need a (leather / new) belt.
9. There was a (large / Persian / red) carpet in the middle of the room.
10. I found this (old / dirty / grey) coat in your room.

137

ORDEN DE LAS PALABRAS. El orden de ciertas palabras en la frase puede cambiar el sentido. Dígase lo que significan las siguientes frases de acuerdo con la colocación de las palabras en cursiva.

1. Mavis is *still* standing.
2. Mavis is standing *still*.

3. Tom admires his *only* brother.
4. Tom *only* admires his brother.

5. I left the room without *finishing* the film.
6. I left the room without the film *finishing*.

7. They found the *wounded* soldier.
8. They found the soldier *wounded*.

9. I have *cleaned* my shoes.
10. I have my shoes *cleaned*.

138
ESTILO DIRECTO / INDIRECTO. Escríbanse en estilo indirecto estas frases, p. ej. *Robert said to me, "My bicycle is broken"* **resulta:** *Robert told me that his bicycle was broken.*

1. My brother said to me, "Why are you late?"
2. He said, "Jean has read the novel."
3. Jimmy said, "I am thirsty."
4. The teacher said to Tom, "Be quiet."
5. He asked, "May I go home?"
6. The doctor said to him, "This woman is ill."
7. I said to her, "Bring me the newspaper."
8. They said, "We'll come tomorrow."
9. I said to him, "Don't forget to post the letter."
10. He said to me, "Get up at seven."

139
ESTILO DIRECTO / INDIRECTO. Para cada oración en estilo directo, constrúyase otra en estilo indirecto, eligiendo las palabras correctas en cada caso.

1. They told me about that.
   He said he (is / was / had been) told about it.
2. I'm sure she doesn't know!
   I explained that I (am / was / have been) sure that she (did / didn't / doesn't) know.
3. Those shoes were repaired a week ago.
   We explained that those shoes (have been / were / had been) repaired the week (ago / before / past).

4. That's a lovely dress you're wearing!
   Mike told her that it (is / were / was) a lovely dress that she (was / have been / had been) wearing.
5. Why didn't you come to class on time?
   The teacher asked the student why he (didn't / wasn't / hadn't) gone to class on time.
6. Let's go to the cinema tonight.
   Jenny suggested that we (went / shouldn't go / did) to the cinema (tonight / that night / then)
7. What do you think of my painting?
   The artist asked what they (think / thought / were thinking) about his painting.
8. How did you do it?
   She asked us how we (did / had done / have done) it.

140

EXCLAMACIONES. Escójase la expresión apropiada:

What   What a   What an   How

1. .... big car!
2. .... hot water!
3. .... difficult question!
4. .... easy it is!
5. .... fair hair he has!
6. .... large family!
7. .... clever they are!
8. .... old church!
9. .... pretty she is!
10. .... interesting!

ANSWER KEY

Ejercicio 1: 1 a; 2 a; 3 x; 4 a; 5 a; 6 a; 7 x; 8 x; 9 a; 10 an; 11 x; 12 a; 13 x; 14 x; 15 an; 16 x; 17 a; 18 a; 19 x; 20 an.

Ejercicio 2: 1 x; 2 x; 3 the; 4 the; 5 x; 6 the; 7 the; 8 x; 9 the; 10 x; 11 the; 12 x; 13 x; 14 x; 15 x; 16 the; 17 x; 18 x; 19 the; 20 the.

Ejercicio 3: 1 x; 2 the; 3 a; 4 an; 5 a; 6 a; 7 the; 8 x; 9 x; 10 x; 11 x; 12 a; 13 x; 14 a; 15 x; 16 x; 17 the; 18 x; 19 the; 20 the / a.

Ejercicio 4: 1 nephew; 2 father; 3 waiter; 4 lion; 5 uncle; 6 man - wizard; 7 brother; 8 gentleman; 9 grandfather.

Ejercicio 5:
1. The queen is speaking now.
2. She is a heroine.
3. The maidservant is there.
4. My wife is sitting on that chair.
5. The girls are waiting.
6. She is a widow.
7. My mother is speaking to the landlady.
8. This is my aunt and this is her daughter.
9. The countess was born here.
10. There are two cows on that farm.

Ejercicio 6: 1 mistress; 2 nephew; 3 actress; 4 tiger; 5 goddess; 6 friar / monk; 7 lass; 8 cock; 9 bride; 10 prince.

Ejercicio 7: 1 brothers-in-law; 2 armchairs; 3 oases; 4 phenomena; 5 women students; 6 children; 7 teeth; 8 safes; 9 thieves; 10 armies; 11 pianos; 12 potatoes; 13 bridges; 14 dishes; 15 heroes; 16 photos; 17 keys; 18 lives; 19 roofs; 20 geese.

Ejercicio 8: No cambian en plural: salmon, sheep, deer, trout.

Ejercicio 9: 1 A bird flies; 2 A boy plays; 3 A dog barks; 4 A cow gives milk; 5 A cat has four legs; 6 A baker sells bread; 7 A horse gallops; 8 A postman delivers letters; 9 A child cries; 10 A man goes to work.

Ejercicio 10:
1. There are some pianos in that room.
2. Look, there are some flies on the ceiling.
3. The knives are on that table.
4. The men came with their wives.

5. My children have just come home from school.
6. I can see some sheep in that field.
7. The watches were in the box.
8. The oxen were near the farm.
9. The books are on those shelves.
10. I've caught some trout.
11. The boy sent some letters without any stamps on them.
12. Are these glasses?
13. Are there any ladies in the shop?
14. Those boys want to go to Liverpool.
15. These are mice.

Ejercicio 11: 1 dining-room; 2 bookcase; 3 teacup; 4 pickpocket; 5 newspaper; 6 shop window; 7 lipstick; 8 housewife; 9 shoe-shop; 10 fortune-teller.

Ejercicio 12:
1. I'm going to give you some advice / I'm going to give you a piece of advice.
2. There's not much furniture in that room.
3. Tom has made some progress in Spanish.
4. I have some interesting news for you. / I have an interesting piece of news for you.
5. Learning English is hard work.
6. I had some buttered toast for breakfast.
7. My sister has a good command of German / My sister has a good knowledge of German.

Ejercicio 13: 1 blind; 2 poor; 3 sick; 4 ambitious; 5 English - French; 6 Welsh; 7 rich; 8 dumb.

Ejercicio 14: 1 longer; 2 hotter; 3 bigger; 4 older; 5 stronger; 6 better; 7 easier; 8 colder; 9 thinner; 10 heavier.

Ejercicio 15: 1 prettiest; 2 more intelligent; 3 as comfortable; 4 longer; 5 warmer; 6 worst; 7 as tall; 8 best; 9 most important; 10 better.

Ejercicio 16:
1. John is as old as James / James is as old as John.
2. The river is as long as the road / The road is as long as the river.
3. Charles is taller than Tony / Tony is not as tall as Charles.
4. The park is bigger than the field.
5. The piano is as heavy as the box / The box is as heavy as the piano.
6. Mr Carter is the richest of the three men.
7. Moon Street is the longest of the three streets.
8. The river is the widest (of the three).

9. The river is deeper than the pond.
10. This car is faster than that motorcycle.

Ejercicio 17: 1 heavier than; 2 as heavy as; 3 not as heavy as; 4 lighter than; 5 the lightest; 6 more expensive than; 7 less expensive than; 8 the most expensive; 9 cheaper than; 10 the cheapest.

Ejercicio 18: 1 tall; 2 long; 3 white; 4 dirty; 5 clean; 6 dead; 7 back; 8 fat; 9 old; 10 cold.

Ejercicio 19:
1. My father is a very absent-minded man.
2. Jack is a very hard-working boy.
3. He was wearing a dark-blue suit.
4. A well-dressed woman came into the room and sat down.
5. There's a dirty-looking boy waiting for you.

Ejercicio 20: 1 them; 2 We; 3 She; 4 me; 5 her; 6 us; 7 They; 8 us; 9 They; 10 we; 11 him; 12 I - me; 13 it; 14 you; 15 us.

Ejercicio 21:
1. They go to school.
2. I was in front of her.
3. He is a very good doctor.
4. She is in the dining-room.
5. The teacher is among them.
6. We are students.
7. It is in the car park.
8. I am behind him.
9. Send us as many books as you can.
10. Where are they?
11. I saw them yesterday.
12. Give her a cup of tea.
13. Put them on the table.
14. Put it on the table.
15. When is he going to visit her?

Ejercicio 22: 1 We - them; 2 I - him; 3 She - us; 4 him; 5 They - us - her; 6 her; 7 me; 8 him; 9 he; 10 They.

Ejercicio 23: 1 ours; 2 hers; 3 yours; 4 mine; 5 theirs; 6 hers; 7 theirs; 8 his; 9 theirs; 10 his.

Ejercicio 24: 1 himself; 2 yourself; 3 myself; 4 themselves; 5 yourselves; 6 herself; 7 itself; 8 myself; 9 yourselves; 10 yourself; 11 himself; 12 one another / each other; 13 one another / each other; 14 one another / each other; 15 one another / each other.

Ejercicio 25: 1 Who; 2 What; 3 Who / Whom; 4 Whose; 5 Which; 6 What; 7 Whose; 8 Which; 9 Who; 10 Who / Whom.

Ejercicio 26:
1. Whose is this bicycle? / Whose bicycle is this?
2. Who is here today?
3. What have you written the letter with?
4. Who did you see at the station?
5. Which of these blouses do you like best? / Which blouse do you like best?
6. Who played in the garden?
7. What did you buy?
8. Who helped you?
9. Whose is this cap? / Whose cap is this?
10. What shall we do now?

Ejercicio 27:
1. Who did he speak to? / Whom did he speak to?
2. What did you open the tin with?
3. Which of these hotels did they go to?
4. Who did you go to the theatre with? / Whom did you go to the theatre with?
5. What are you talking about?
6. Who did you send the letter to? / Whom did you send the letter to?
7. What is the thinking about?
8. Who did he look at? / Whom did he look at?
9. Who did you receive those flowers from? / Whom did you receive those flowers from?
10. Who are you waiting for? / Whom are you waiting for?

Ejercicio 28:
1. The dog which is barking is not mine.
2. The woman who is singing is Mrs Williams.
3. The parrot which is speaking is beautiful.
4. The boy who broke the window is my cousin.
5. The cat which always sleeps in that basket belongs to Mrs Carter / The cat which belongs to Mrs Carter always sleeps in that basket.
6. The students who study geography are in that classroom / The students who are in that classroom study geography.
7. The traveller who tells interesting stories is very old.
8. The man who lives here now travelled all over the world / The man who travelled all over the world lives here now.
9. The station-master who has a blue cap stopped the train / The station-master who stopped the train has a blue cap.

10. The horse which won the race last week is white.

Ejercicio 29: 1 x; 2 x; 3 which; 4 who; 5 which; 6 who; 7 who; 8 x; 9 which; 10 which.

Ejercicio 30:
1. These are the fishermen we always talk to.
2. Those are the fishing-boats they were speaking about.
3. That's the bus I go to school in.
4. This is the picture I am looking at.
5. That's the man I lent the money to.
6. This is the hotel we stayed in.
7. That's the glass he used to drink wine from.
8. Those are the ladies my sister lives with.
9. This is the record I listened to.
10. That's the chair he sat on.

Ejercicio 31:
1. The sheep in that field give good wool.
2. The swans on the pond are very beautiful.
3. The horse under that tree is eating grass.
4. The man by the traffic lights is a policeman.
5. The students in that classroom are studying French.
6. The vase on that table is very fragile.
7. The car in the garage is mine.
8. The apples in that basket are ripe.
9. The children in the park are playing football.
10. The glasses in the cupboard are dirty.
11. The shirt on the bed is mine.
12. The tickets in this envelope are for you.

Ejercicio 32: 1 nothing - anything; 2 anyone - nobody; 3 something - anything; 4 something - nothing; 5 anyone - nobody; 6 Some; 7 nobody; 8 Anything.

Ejercicio 33: 1 anything; 2 nothing; 3 nobody; 4 something; 5 anything; 6 something; 7 Everyone; 8 One; 9 nothing; 10 nothing.

Ejercicio 34: 1 ... and the blue one is here; 2 ... and that's a mild one; 3 ... and that one is big; 4 ..., good ones and bad ones; 5 ... Fill the empty one; 6 ... or the one by the window?; 7 ... No, I wore the new one; 8 ... Did you see the one they showed last week?; 9 ... She likes brown ones; 10 ... as the ones your brother took last year.

Ejercicio 35: 1 her; 2 your; 3 her; 4 my; 5 your; 6 hers; 7 his; 8 mine; 9 Our; 10 its; 11 mine; 12 theirs; 13 hers; 14 ours; 15 his; 16 your; 17 its; 18 their; 19 my; 20 her.

Ejercicio 36: 1 her; 2 you; 3 my; 4 his; 5 me; 6 themselves; 7 herself; 8 ours; 9 you; 10 him.

Ejercicio 37: 1 each (adjetivo); 2 little (adjetivo); 3 few (adjetivo); 4 All (adjetivo); 5 much (adjetivo); 6 both (pronombre); 7 most (pronombre); 8 few (pronombre); 9 Few (adjetivo); 10 much (adjetivo); 11 another (pronombre); 12 another (adjetivo); 13 others (pronombre); 14 neither (pronombre); 15 either (adjetivo).

Ejercicio 38:
1. You haven't much fish on your plate. / You don't have much fish on your plate. / You haven't got much fish on your plate.
2. She hasn't told me the news.
3. They didn't come last night.
4. She didn't buy any bread this morning.
5. I don't want to go abroad for my holidays.
6. They didn't study French last year.
7. He doesn't catch a bus to go to work.
8. We aren't going to eat meat for lunch.
9. I don't think she's intelligent.
10. He hasn't (got) many friends in London. / He doesn't have many friends in London.

Ejercicio 39:
1. Are they going to leave at ten o'clock?
2. Did he catch a bus this morning?
3. Does she study her lessons in the afternoon?
4. Did my father eat any fish for lunch?
5. Did your mother buy any sweets for Betty?
6. Does he understand me?
7. Does my sister come to class every day?
8. Does he smoke a pipe after lunch?
9. Has your brother (got) many friends in this town? / Does your brother have many friends in this town?
10. Does Mr Evans eat much meat?

Ejercicio 40:
1. Can he speak English?
2. Did she come last week?
3. Does he know her?
4. Have you seen them?
5. Did you catch the bus this morning?
6. Are you Spanish?
7. Did they see you at the station?
8. Have you got any money?

9. Did you stop the car by the bank?
10. Do you smoke?

Ejercicio 41:
1. What's this pencil for?
2. What are you interested in?
3. Who does this dog belong to?
4. Where does he come from?
5. When did you see him?
6. What shall we have for lunch?
7. Why won't he come today?
8. What's she studying?
9. Where did you put the book?
10. At what time did they come? / What time did they come?

Ejercicio 42: 1 Put; 2 Speak; 3 Drive; 4 Take; 5 Get; 6 Wash; 7 Type; 8 Lend; 9 Knock; 10 Close.

Ejercicio 43:
1. They're learning English.
2. He's drinking a cup of tea.
3. She's reading a novel.
4. I'm telephoning Mr Field.
5. The girls are playing with dolls.
6. The dog is eating a bone.
7. We're watching television.
8. Philip is sitting an exam.
9. I'm putting on my coat.
10. My sister is playing the violin.

Ejercicio 44:
1. Dick has played chess.
2. John has read a book.
3. I have found my bag.
4. David has spoken English.
5. She has told us the truth.
6. My father has smoked a pipe.
7. They have bought a new flat.
8. He has walked along the street.
9. I have lost my money.
10. Your sister has eaten a cake.

Ejercicio 45: 1 drink - aren't drinking; 2 Are you selling?; 3 understand; 4 are wearing; 5 rains; 6 is raining; 7 are you doing; 8 do you do; 9 wears; 10 floats; 11 am going; 12 is coming; 13 go; 14 ask; 15 sleeps.

Ejercicio 46: 1 bought; 2 wrote; 3 has lived; 4 was listening - went, 5 has lived; 6 were having - rang; 7 received; 8 opened; 9 has been; 10 haven't seen; 11 hasn't finished; 12 played; 13 stayed; 14 I have already seen; 15 has drunk.

Ejercicio 47: 1 bought; 2 Have you counted; 3 was not; 4 are watching; 5 found; 6 go; 7 spoken; 8 has been; 9 came; 10 shine; 11 was; 12 see; 13 is having; 14 reads; 15 read; 16 is speaking; 17 is raining; 18 They have just arrived; 19 have lived; 20 When did you come; 21 Did you buy; 22 don't know; 23 hasn't worked; 24 doesn't speak; 25 studies.

Ejercicio 48: 1 sneezed; 2 bit; 3 knocked; 4 began; 5 met; 6 was writing; 7 was shaving; 8 were having; 9 were walking; 10 was waiting.

Ejercicio 49: 1 came - was snowing; 2 studied; 3 played; 4 came - was working; 5 began; 6 were shouting - entered; 7 was speaking - knocked; 8 arrived - was already giving; 9 had finished; 10 robbed.

Ejercicio 50:
1. I was writing a letter.
2. He was playing cards.
3. She was going to work.
4. They were playing in the garden.
5. She was making a cake.
6. She was sleeping.
7. She / He was explaining the lesson.
8. He was reading the newspaper.
9. I was having a bath.
10. They were working.

Ejercicio 51: 1 ..., she had already cooked lunch; 2 ..., Mr Wilson had already left; 3 ..., the film had already started; 4 ..., the train had already gone; 5 ..., I had already bought the newspaper; 6 ..., he had already done his homework; 7 ..., the manager had already called him; 8 ..., I had already peeled the potatoes; 9 ..., he had already studied English; 10 ... that I had already seen it.

Ejercicio 52: 1 will be; 2 will find; 3 will never do; 4 will do; 5 shall be / will be; 6 shall go / will go; 7 will see; 8 shall telephone / will telephone; 9 will close; 10 shan't be / won't be.

Ejercicio 53: 1 work; 2 worked; 3 had; 4 will explode; 5 would have got; 6 would have bought; 7 had sent; 8 rained; 9 rains; 10 will catch.

Ejercicio 54:
1. But if he had had money, he could have bought a motorbike.
2. But if they had had a car, they wouldn't have had to go by bus.

3. But if we had worked, we would have earned money.
4. But if I had seen him, I would have told him.
5. But if I had won the lottery, I could have bought the house I wanted.
6. But if we had finished the work on time, we would have got a bonus.
7. But if he had studied hard, he would have got good marks in the test.
8. But if they had parked on the yellow line, they would have been given a fine.
9. But if she had remembered to post the letter, it would have arrived before Friday.
10. But if he had forgotten to buy his wife a birthday present, she would have been angry.
11. But if I had set the alarm clock, I wouldn't have overslept.
12. But if we had worn overcoats, we wouldn't have felt very cold.

Ejercicio 55:
1. I told you to come.
2. I'll give you some money so (that) you may go to the cinema. / I'll give you some money so (that) you can go to the cinema.
3. I am surprised (that) Tony should come so early today.
4. It is important for us to go there together. / It is important that we go there together.
5. He says (that) he will tell her when she comes.
6. He said (that) he would tell her when she came.
7. I wish I knew!
8. I want to have my hair cut / I want them to cut my hair.
9. This lesson is too difficult for her to understand.
10. As soon as Dorothy arrives, tell her (that) I found her book.

Ejercicio 56:
1. I always shave in the morning.
2. John and Molly love each other. / John and Molly love one another.
3. Those three men hate one another. / Those three men hate each other.
4. She is looking at herself in the mirror.
5. Come in and sit down.
6. I cut myself with this knife.
7. We got lost in London.
8. When I work hard I get tired.
9. Don't worry.
10. Are you getting off at the next stop?

Ejercicio 57: 1 used to; 2 can't / couldn't; 3 should / must / ought to; 4 can; 5 can't / couldn't; 6 must / should / ought to; 7 used to; 8 must; 9 can't; 10 needn't; 11 can't; 12 must; 13 must; 14 can't; 15 may / can; 16 mustn't / shouldn't; 17 couldn't; 18 must; 19 may / might; 20 needn't; 21 couldn't; 22 mustn't; 23 Can; 24 might / could; 25 would; 26 would; 27 will; 28 Shall / May; 29 should / ought to; 30 Will / Would.

Ejercicio 58:   1 did it?;   2 is it?;   3 don't they?;   4 aren't I?;   5 don't we?;   6 do you?;   7 have they?;   8 won't he?;   9 could I?;   10 hasn't he? / doesn't he?

Ejercicio 59:   1 understand;   2 make;   3 buy;   4 go;   5 hear;   6 cut;   7 go;   8 write;   9 smoke;   10 listen;   11 go;   12 type.

Ejercicio 60:   1 must;   2 can;   3 needn't;   4 would;   5 had been;   6 shouldn't;   7 can't;   8 ought to;   9 should;   10 Shall;   11 Shall;   12 can't;   13 must;   14 mustn't;   15 Will.

Ejercicio 61:   1 There is;   2 There may be / There might be;   3 Is there;   4 There are;   5 There was;   6 There were;   7 There will be;   8 There is;   9 There will be;   10 There was;   11 There were;   12 There will be;   13 There is;   14 Is there;   15 There is.

Ejercicio 62:   1 see;   2 bit;   3 blow;   4 spelt (también spelled);   5 came;   6 sent;   7 rises;   8 became;   9 found;   10 leave;   11 heard;   12 swam.

Ejercicio 63:   1 ate;   2 bought;   3 drank;   4 built;   5 seen;   6 told;   7 cut;   8 put;   9 sold;   10 heard.

Ejercicio 64:   1 drank;   2 go;   3 writes;   4 began;   5 spoken;   6 given;   7 sings;   8 done;   9 saw;   10 forgotten;   11 been;   12 broke;   13 taken;   14 eat;   15 bite.

Ejercicio 65:   1 up;   2 on;   3 off;   4 up;   5 in;   6 up;   7 up;   8 down;   9 on;   10 on;   11 down;   12 back;   13 on;   14 up;   15 down.

Ejercicio 66:   1 for;   2 on;   3 off;   4 for;   5 out;   6 in;   7 for;   8 for;   9 in;   10 out;   11 on;   12 off;   13 back;   14 out;   15 up.

Ejercicio 67:   1 Switch off / turn off;   2 Run into / come across;   3 Fill in / fill out;   4 Walk off / walk away;   5 Bring up / throw up;   6 Run off / run away;   7 Call up / ring up;   8 Put off / put back;   9 Think up / make up;   10 Throw away / throw out.

Ejercicio 68:   1 b;   2 a;   3 c;   4 c;   5 a;   6 b; 7 a;   8 b;   9 c;   10 b; 11 a;   12 c.

Ejercicio 69:   1 to go;   2 to spend;   3 bathe;   4 have;   5 to go;   6 to get;   7 to eat;   8 work;   9 to learn;   10 to translate;   11 to speak;   12 to telephone;   13 lift;   14 come;   15 to stand up.

Ejercicio 70:   1 to;   2 x;   3 x;   4 to;   5 x;   6 to;   7 to;   8 x;   9 to;   10 to;   11 to;   12 to;   13 x;   14 x;   15 to.

Ejercicio 71:
1. Painting is interesting.
2. Spelling English words isn't easy.

3. Walking is good exercise.
4. Driving a car at full speed is dangerous.
5. Winning a prize is very difficult.
6. Choosing presents for Christmas takes a long time.
7. Eating is necessary for everybody.
8. Playing the piano is marvellous.
9. Working hard is tiring.
10. Learning languages is necessary nowadays.

Ejercicio 72: 1 talking; 2 drinking; 3 seeing; 4 reading; 5 working; 6 laughing; 7 stealing; 8 going; 9 hearing; 10 writing.

Ejercicio 73: 1 saying; 2 reading; 3 drawing; 4 teaching; 5 taking; 6 travelling; 7 wasting; 8 coming; 9 watching; 10 going.

Ejercicio 74: 1 speaking; 2 living; 3 bathing; 4 smoking; 5 writing; 6 watching; 7 going; 8 playing; 9 driving; 10 having.

Ejercicio 75: 1 to rain / raining; 2 go; 3 going; 4 work; 5 to do; 6 to work / working; 7 to paint; 8 to snow / snowing; 9 sending; 10 to do; 11 to stay; 12 to scrub / scrubbing.

Ejercicio 76: 1 singing; 2 to speak; 3 to read; 4 drinking; 5 eat; 6 visiting; 7 translating; 8 travelling; 9 closing; 10 to understand; 11 stay; 12 trying; 13 do; 14 to see; 15 play.

Ejercicio 77: 1 to; 2 x; 3 x; 4 x; 5 to; 6 x; 7 to; 8 to; 9 to; 10 to; 11 x; 12 x; 13 to; 14 x; 15 x; 16 to; 17 to; 18 to; 19 to; 20 x.

Ejercicio 78:
1. The classroom is being painted.
2. The lost child was found.
3. My dictionary has been stolen.
4. The letters will be typed.
5. Mr Wilson was rescued.
6. The dishes should be washed.
7. The wheel must be changed.
8. The rope was lowered.
9. The parcels were sent to Spain.

Ejercicio 79:
1. I was promised a new job.
2. She was shown some nice ties.
3. He was asked three questions.
4. She was taught how to play the piano.

5. I was offered a cup of tea.
6. They were told the results of the exam.
7. I was given a watch as a present.
8. Pat was paid the money he had earned.
9. I was asked to leave.
10. We were made to work hard.
11. You were told to speak more slowly.
12. I was advised to be silent.

Ejercicio 80:   1 use;   2 used to;   3 isn't used to;   4 are used;   5 used;   6 used;   7 Did / Didn't - use;   8 used to;   9 did - use;   10 use;   11 didn't use to;   12 wasn't used to;   13 is used to - isn't used to;   14 used to - not used to;   15 use to;   16 used to;   17 used to - use;   18 used to;   19 use to.

Ejercicio 81:   1 had it repaired;   2 have it installed;   3 has them typed;   4 has them pressed;   5 had it made;   6 had them paid;   7 have it cleaned;   8 have them made;   9 has them made;   10 have it tested;   11 had it checked;   12 had them repaired.

Ejercicio 82:   1 make;   2 made;   3 does;   4 doing;   5 Do;   6 making;   7 make;   8 doing;   9 do;   10 do;   11 Make;   12 did;   13 do;   14 make;   15 do.

Ejercicio 83:
1. He never reads in bed.
2. I seldom write with my father's pen.
3. He is always ready to tell them stories.
4. The girl doesn't always help her mother.
5. His hands are often dirty.
6. You aren't usually ready.
7. I sometimes go to the cinema in the evening.
8. Does she usually cook lunch?
9. They generally come in the morning.
10. My cousin came two hours ago.
11. Philip has just broken the vase.
12. Have you ever been to London?
13. She has never come in the morning.
14. Betty sometimes drinks milk.
15. I have already seen that programme.
16. Has she arrived yet?
17. They are still asleep.
18. Did she ever ask for their help?
19. I haven't had breakfast yet.
20. My parents often go to the theatre in the evening.

Ejercicio 84:   1 a;   2 b;   3 a;   4 b;   5 c;   6 b;   7 a;   8 b;   9 b;   10 a.

Ejercicio 85:
1. I had completely forgotten the time.
2. She smokes too much.
3. The lift operates automatically.
4. The secretary opens the mail in the morning.
5. We read that magazine every week.
6. She telephones me in the afternoon.
7. This book is extremely interesting.
8. He will return the dictionary next week.
9. Betty is easily tired.
10. The work was badly done / The work was done badly.

Ejercicio 86: 1 He timidly invited me...; 2 The man sarcastically said that...; 3 We emphatically requested him...; 4 She insistently told the boy...; 5 That boy shrewdly observed that...; 6 She wisely answered what she...; 7 She politely asked them...; 8 I carefully explained to them...; 9 Your brother rudely ordered me...; 10 Joan boastfully told us...

Ejercicio 87: 1 ... in a drawer yesterday; 2 ... in one of my classes this month; 3 ... in class last week; 4 ... very fast last night; 5 ... very well now; 6 ... at university this year; 7 ... at the Capitol last month; 8 ... there once; 9 ... very well last night; 10 ... slowly now.

Ejercicio 88: 1 ... all the cakes at the party yesterday; 2 ... this picture very carefully a week ago; 3 ... the tree very well in class; 4 ... to school by bus in the morning; 5 ... my trousers very well a week ago; 6 ... a lot of sandwiches at the party; 7 ... this tie cheaply last Wednesday; 8 ... football in the park in summer; 9 ... dinner in the kitchen at seven o'clock.

Ejercicio 89: 1 ... carefully in the office; 2 ...slowly along the street; 3 ...fluently in class; 4 ...fast along the road; 5 ...reluctantly on Mondays; 6 ...quickly in his office; 7 ...bravely in the war; 8 ... noisily in the park; 9 ...politely at the meeting; 10 ...very well on that table.

Ejercicio 90: 1 ...very carefully yesterday; 2 ...very slowly this afternoon; 3 ...frankly last night; 4 ...calmly a week ago; 5 ...clearly a month ago; 6 ...tirelessly from Monday to Friday; 7 ...distinctly last Sunday; 8 ...enthusiastically last year; 9 ...nicely every day; 10 ...quickly on Friday.

Ejercicio 91: 1 ...in the street on Tuesday; 2 ...at that factory last year; 3 ...in the park on Sundays; 4 ...at a restaurant every day; 5 ...in London last week; 6 ...in a hotel tomorrow; 7 ...on that wall a week ago; 8 ...in the office this morning; 9 ...in this room this afternoon; 10 ...here yesterday.

Ejercicio 92: 1 ...slowly in the park in the afternoons; 2 ...very happily here every day; 3 ...very emphatically at the meeting last week; 4 ...very quickly in class every day; 5 ...very carefully in your office at once; 6 ...quietly in the playground yesterday; 7 ...slowly in class tomorrow?; 8 ...very noisily in that room at this moment; 9 ...slowly in the beginners' class on Tuesdays.

Ejercicio 93:
1. Where do they live?
2. When did you write it?
3. How did she come?
4. Why did they run?
5. Where did you hit the thief?
6. Why have you come?
7. How are you?
8. When will he come?
9. Where did she go?
10. Why is he learning English?

Ejercicio 94:
1. I read more quickly than Bruce / I read faster than Bruce I read quicker than Bruce.
2. Tony is the boy who runs fastest.
3. This car isn't big enough for us.
4. I only have eighty pounds.
5. The tea is too hot.
6. The bus was quite full / The bus was completely full.
7. This is the best wine I have ever drunk.
8. I have a car, too / I also have a car.
9. As a doctor he is quite good / He is quite good as a doctor.
10. Do you want anything else? / Would you like anything else?
11. This hat is too big for me.
12. If you work hard, you'll earn more money.
13. I like apples very much.
14. Two pounds is too much (to pay) for this ball-pen.
15. He's not going and I'm not going either.
16. Tony speaks Spanish very badly.
17. He can hardly write.
18. This perfume smells nice.

Ejercicio 95: 1 yet - not yet; 2 ago - since; 3 now - still; 4 ago - yet - still; 5 yet - now; 6 still - ago; 7 still - already - ago.

Ejercicio 96: 1 clever - cleverly; 2 carefully - careful; 3 good - well; 4 patiently - patient; 5 fluent - fluently; 6 good - well; 7 well - good; 8 dangerous - dangerously.

Ejercicio 97: 1 enough; 2 too; 3 too - enough; 4 enough; 5 too; 6 enough; 7 enough; 8 enough; 9 enough; 10 too; 11 too - enough; 12 enough - too; 13 enough - too; 14 too; 15 enough.

Ejercicio 98: 1 such; 2 such; 3 so - such; 4 such - so; 5 such; 6 such; 7 so; 8 so; 9 such; 10 such; 11 so.

Ejercicio 99: 1 for; 2 to; 3 for; 4 to; 5 to; 6 for; 7 for; 8 to; 9 for; 10 to.

Ejercicio 100: 1 at; 2 in; 3 at; 4 in; 5 at; 6 in; 7 in; 8 in; 9 at; 10 at.

Ejercicio 101: 1 during; 2 for; 3 for; 4 during; 5 for; 6 during; 7 for; 8 for; 9 during; 10 for.

Ejercicio 102: 1 between; 2 between; 3 among; 4 among; 5 among; 6 between; 7 among / between; 8 between; 9 between; 10 between / among.

Ejercicio 103: 1 for; 2 since; 3 since; 4 for; 5 since; 6 for; 7 since; 8 for; 9 since; 10 for; 11 since; 12 for.

Ejercicio 104: 1 from; 2 from; 3 of; 4 from; 5 of; 6 of; 7 of; 8 from; 9 of; 10 from.

Ejercicio 105: 1 in; 2 on; 3 on; 4 in; 5 on; 6 on; 7 in; 8 on; 9 in; 10 on.

Ejercicio 106: 1 into; 2 in; 3 into; 4 into; 5 in; 6 in; 7 to; 8 to; 9 into; 10 in.

Ejercicio 107: 1 in; 2 at; 3 at; 4 on; 5 in; 6 at; 7 in; 8 at; 9 in; 10 at.

Ejercicio 108: 1 along; 2 at; 3 at; 4 on; 5 by; 6 in; 7 for; 8 on; 9 at; 10 at.

Ejercicio 109: 1 for; 2 by; 3 into; 4 along; 5 on; 6 on; 7 by; 8 on; 9 in; 10 on.

Ejercicio 110: 1 with; 2 at; 3 between; 4 on; 5 from; 6 for; 7 at; 8 to; 9 for; 10 for.

Ejercicio 111: 1 with; 2 in; 3 to; 4 for; 5 at; 6 to; 7 of; 8 with; 9 of; 10 without.

Ejercicio 112: 1 at / in; 2 for; 3 for; 4 on; 5 on (visitar) / for (ir a buscar); 6 on; 7 at; 8 in / at; 9 to; 10 for / to.

Ejercicio 113: 1 at; 2 to; 3 on; 4 from; 5 for; 6 at; 7 to; 8 at; 9 of; 10 of.

Ejercicio 114: 1 to; 2 in; 3 for; 4 from; 5 with; 6 for; 7 at; 8 at; 9 at / in; 10 in an hour (dentro de una hora) / for an hour (durante una hora); 11 in; 12 at.

Ejercicio 115: 1 on - in; 2 at - at; 3 over - in; 4 on - in; 5 on - over; 6 at / in - over; 7 in - at; 8 in - on; 9 at - at; 10 at - at.

Ejercicio 116: 1 from - to - by; 2 of - on / from - of; 3 at - of - to; 4 at - on - of; 5 to - of - by / from; 6 to - for - on; 7 of - to - in / at; 8 to - to - of; 9 at - on - of; 10 to - about - in.

Ejercicio 117: 1 in; 2 about (¿de quién estás hablando?) / to (¿a quién estás hablando?); 3 to; 4 at (¿qué miras?) / for (¿qué buscas?); 5 on; 6 about; 7 of; 8 from; 9 in; 10 for.

Ejercicio 118: 1 with; 2 in; 3 from; 4 of / about; 5 to (con quien hablaste) / about (de quien hablaste); 6 about; 7 in / at; 8 from; 9 in; 10 with; 11 to; 12 in; 13 on; 14 on.

Ejercicio 119:
1. The teacher said, "Write an essay about anything you like." / "Write an essay on anything you like."
2. The boy was going along the street when it began to rain.
3. This book was written by my father.
4. This is different from silk.
5. We did it for a joke.
6. I bought it for ten pounds.
7. I am ashamed of you.
8. I'm tired of working.
9. There's a fly on the ceiling.
10. This is the only cinema in town.

Ejercicio 120: 1 and; 2 whether; 3 what; 4 that; 5 where; 6 that; 7 that; 8 that; 9 when; 10 what; 11 whether; 12 and.

Ejercicio 121: 1 that; 2 so; 3 When; 4 because; 5 Although; 6 that; 7 if; 8 that; 9 till; 10 As.

Ejercicio 122:
1. I know a girl who has two brothers.
2. There isn't much water, so we can't wash.
3. I've brought these two cases because Charles couldn't carry them all.
4. We sell books and magazines.
5. When I arrived at the station, the train had left.
6. Though I was tired, I didn't stop walking.
7. Neither you nor I can do it.
8. The cap (that) I bought in London is very nice.
9. As I was in a hurry, I caught a plane.
10. He gave me what I wanted.

Ejercicio 123:
1. Will you answer the telephone, as you are nearest?
2. I taught David and David taught Tony.
3. He hasn't much money, but he has a lot of friends. / He doesn't have much money, but he's got a lot of friends.
4. Put your coat on if you're cold.
5. Neither you nor I can do it.
6. We don't know if it's right or not / We don't know whether it's right or not.
7. John says (that) he has a lot of money. / John says (that) he has got a lot of money.
8. Although I did the work very carefully, she did not like the result.
9. Pronounce this word as you have been taught.
10. The girl looked at us as though she understood us.

Ejercicio 124: 1 where; 2 although; 3 when; 4 when; 5 before; 6 so that; 7 unless; 8 because / as; 9 as; 10 where; 11 unless; 12 if; 13 although; 14 Although.

Ejercicio 125:
1. This is the teacher's book.
2. That is Mary's bag.
3. Those are the students' books.
4. This is my friend's umbrella.
5. That is your sister's hat.
6. These are your brothers' coins.
7. That is the waiters' money.
8. Those are my children's ball-pens.
9. That is the waiter's money.
10. That is the bell-boy's uniform.

Ejercicio 126:
1. Jane's and Betty's friends.
2. Jane and Betty's friends.
3. Have you ever been to St Mark's?
4. Today we are going to my brother's (house).
5. The leg of the table.
6. The honesty of the poor.
7. These are the clothes of the boys who are playing football.
8. I'm a friend of Jack's.
9. This car is Philip's.
10. Whose is this car? / Whose car is this? -It's Tony's.

Ejercicio 127: 1 So is Mary; 2 So do I; 3 So can they; 4 Neither did we; 5 So does my father; 6 Neither is he; 7 I didn't either; 8 He couldn't either; 9 Neither do my parents; 10 Neither have we.

Ejercicio 128:
1. The blue car is on sale.
2. The man with (the) grey hair is a French driver / The Frenchman with (the) grey hair is a driver.
3. Mr Grey has read a lot of books on phonetics.
4. The girl who has the yellow dress on is from Germany.
5. The boy in the red sweater, who is talking to Pam, is Jim's friend.
6. Please find my mother a taxi.
7. The men wearing blue uniforms are policemen.
8. Philip is always in a hurry because he never gets up on time.
9. He often reads the paper in the morning.
10. He has never been to Belgium before.
11. I want to buy a good antique table.
12. Betty is a pretty young girl.

Ejercicio 129: 1 ...where Arthur is; 2 ...what time it is?; 3 ...was an old house; 4 ...is a box; 5 ...what he is doing; 6 ...how you did it; 7 ...this letter for me; 8 ...a chair for Wendy; 9 ...Wendy a chair; 10 ...the lesson to them.

Ejercicio 130:
1. He spoke Russian very well.
2. She flew to London on the morning plane.
3. You must tighten the rope firmly.
4. I've never been there.
5. The letter was badly written.
6. His work was carefully done.
7. She speaks English badly.
8. I sometimes go there / I go there sometimes.
9. You must never say that.
10. I quite understand you.

Ejercicio 131:
1. Toledo is a town famous for its cathedral.
2. There's a sick boy in that bed.
3. The boy is ill today / The boy is sick today.
4. We need somebody intelligent.
5. She dyed her dress red.
6. I found my father wounded.
7. A big silk carpet.
8. A white plastic bag.
9. A big old English ship.
10. An old yellow dress.

Ejercicio 132:
1. My mother liked the play very much.

2. He quickly wrote all the letters (se apresuró a escribir todas las cartas) / He wrote all the letters quickly (escribió todas las cartas rápidamente).
3. He hardly ever reads a newspaper.
4. She never remembers my birthday.
5. I usually finish work at five o'clock.
6. We'll probably go to France next year.
7. Why are you always late?
8. They rarely go to the cinema.
9. It often rains in London.
10. My father only plays tennis on Sundays.

Ejercicio 133: 1 ... that man is; 2 ... it is; 3 ... he was absent; 4 ... the boys are doing; 5 ... they are.

Ejercicio 134:
1. John said goodbye to me.
2. I told a story to the children / I told the children a story.
3. She showed it to them.
4. She made Peter a sandwich / She made a sandwich for Peter.
5. The shopkeeper sold me a jersey / The shopkeeper sold a jersey to me.
6. The shopkeeper sold a jersey to an old woman / The shopkeeper sold an old woman a jersey.
7. I promised a reward to whoever could find my dog / I promised whoever could find my dog a reward.
8. Mr Wilson taught us English / Mr Wilson taught English to us.

Ejercicio 135:
1. I'd like to know what the time is by the clock in the sitting-room.
2. I want to know what your name is.
3. Jack wants to know what the time is.
4. Let's ask that policeman where the park is.
5. Please tell me where the railway station is.
6. Please tell me, where is the railway station?
7. How far is London from here?
8. Do you know how far London is from here?
9. How old is your aunt Joan?
10. I wonder how old your aunt Joan is.

Ejercicio 136:
1. Molly has a new yellow dress.
2. The book is in that blue plastic bag.
3. There is a small square table in that corner.
4. This is a nice silk handkerchief.
5. My father has bought this antique Chinese vase.
6. There was a fat French boy at the party.

7. Tom was carrying a big brown case.
8. I need a new leather belt.
9. There was a large red Persian carpet in the middle of the room.
10. I found this dirty old grey coat in your room.

Ejercicio 137:
1. Mavis está aún de pie.
2. Mavis está de pie sin moverse.

3. Tom admira a su único hermano.
4. Tom admira solamente a su hermano.

5. Salí de la habitación sin terminar la película (el que habla hacía la película).
6. Salí de la habitación sin que terminara la película (el que habla estaba viendo la película).

7. Encontraron al soldado herido (sabían que estaba herido).
8. Encontraron herido al soldado (no sabían que estuviera herido).

9. Me he limpiado los zapatos.
10. Mando los zapatos a limpiar.

Ejercicio 138:
1. My brother asked me why I was late.
2. He said that Jean had read the novel.
3. Jimmy said that he was thirsty.
4. The teacher told Tom to be quiet.
5. He asked if he might go home.
6. The doctor told him (that) that woman was ill.
7. I told her to bring me the newspaper.
8. They said that they would come the following day.
9. I told him not to forget to post the letter.
10. He told me to get up at seven.

Ejercicio 139: 1 had been; 2 was - didn't; 3 had been - before; 4 was - was; 5 hadn't; 6 went - that night; 7 thought; 8 had done.

Ejercicio 140: 1 What a; 2 What; 3 What a; 4 How; 5 What; 6 What a; 7 How; 8 What an; 9 How; 10 How.

NOTES

Anglo-Didáctica Publishing

NOTES

ANGLO-DIDACTICA PUBLISHING

Libros didácticos complementarios

From the same publisher

GRAMMAR & REFERENCE BOOKS

El inglés compendiado. An Easy English Grammar. Manual muy completo, claro, práctico y esquemático de gramática inglesa.

Las preposiciones inglesas y sus ejercicios. La información recopilada en este libro no se encuentra como tal en ningún tratado de gramática. Abundantes frases prácticas, 35 ejercicios y soluciones.

La palabra justa en inglés. Choose your Words Carefully. Se comparan pares de palabras básicas, como Do-Make; Say-Tell, hasta un total de 50 grupos, explicando su uso correcto. Abundantes ejercicios con su clave.

Las dificultades idiomáticas del inglés. Resuelve de manera muy práctica las dificultades que se presentan con mayor frecuencia.

To Get. El verbo comodín del inglés. Estudio completo y sumamente práctico de este verbo. Con 25 ejercicios y soluciones.

EXERCISES & TESTS IN ENGLISH

100 tests para reavivar su inglés. Selección de 100 Tests muy variados, divididos en tres niveles: elemental, intermedio y avanzado. Con soluciones.

Ejercicios de verbos ingleses combinados con partículas. Más de 1.000 ejercicios sobre estos verbos, con soluciones. Complemento de: "Verbos ingleses combinados con partículas".

PRACTICE IN TRANSLATION SPANISH-ENGLISH.

Manual de traducción inversa. Español-inglés. Contiene más de 1.000 ejercicios de traducción del español al inglés, desde la frase al texto. Con alternativas.

Textos literarios para traducir. Español-inglés. Nivel avanzado. Textos literarios de autores contemporáneos de habla española traducidos al inglés con numerosas notas y variantes alternativas. Muy útil para alumnos avanzados y opositores.

Cuaderno para la traducción inversa. Español-inglés. Verbos. Contiene 165 ejercicios de traducción inversa sobre verbos con dificultad para el estudiante español. Unico por las alternativas a todas las traducciones.

SPECIALIZED DICTIONARIES

Catálogo de expresiones para la traducción inversa. Español - inglés. Más de 7.000 expresiones de uso corriente que facilitan tanto la expresión oral como escrita.

Diccionario auxiliar del traductor. Español-inglés. The Translator's Auxiliary Dictionary. Más de 5.000 frases de uso corriente para ilustrar el uso de las palabras del lenguaje cotidiano.

English False Friends. Palabras inglesas engañosas. Selección de palabras inglesas cuyo parecido con otras españolas es motivo de equivocaciones. Con ejercicios y soluciones.

The English Tom, Dick & Harry Speak. Español - inglés. Modismos, dichos y expresiones coloquiales.

English Slang. Inglés - Español. Más de 2.000 expresiones de slang de inglés cotidiano.

Diccionario de dudas del inglés. Diccionario excepcional que analiza y resuelve las dudas del estudiante español.

ENGLISH PRONUNCIATION BOOKS

La pronunciación inglesa. Fonética y fonología. Estudio práctico de los sonidos ingleses. Ilustrado con 50 dibujos y 10 fotos. Con cassette.

Ejercicios de transcripción fonética en inglés. 45 párrafos graduados para practicar la transcripción fonética. Desde la frase al texto. Con notas y soluciones.

Práctica de pronunciación inglesa. English Pronunciation Practice. Contiene 75 ejercicios de entrenamiento auditivo. Con soluciones y transcripción fonética de las palabras.

Fonética funcional inglesa. Manual muy completo y práctico de pronunciación inglesa. Estudio de los sonidos, la acentuación de las palabras, ritmo y entonación. Con ejercicios.

MISCELLANEOUS ENGLISH

Refranes ingleses para estudiantes de inglés. Selección de 500 refranes característicos de la idiosincrasia anglosajona, con su equivalencia española. Libro práctico con notas, ejercicios y soluciones.

Grammar & Humour. Aprenda inglés con una sonrisa. Antología del humor británico. Con breves comentarios gramaticales. Ejercicios y soluciones.

English in Flashes. Más de 300 puntos lingüísticos ingleses de uso corriente y de diversa dificultad.

Juegos de palabras en inglés. Amenísima selección de "piruetas lingüísticas" basadas en el doble sentido de las palabras.

Catálogo Gratuito

Solicite gratuitamente nuestro catálogo completo y totalmente actualizado de Libros Didácticos Complementarios escribiendo a la siguiente dirección, o llamando al teléfono que se indica.

Anglo-Didáctica Publishing
C/ Santiago de Compostela, 16 – bajo B
28034 Madrid
Tel y Fax: 91 378 01 88